KERYGMA
and COMEDY
in the New Testament

KERYGMA

AND COMEDY

In the New Testament

A Structuralist Approach to Hermeneutic

by
DAN O. VIA, Jr.

FORTRESS PRESS   Philadelphia

4405G74   Printed in the United States of Amercia   1-281

To My Mother

and the

Memory of My Father

Contents

Preface

I should like to acknowledge my gratitude to the Society for Religion in Higher Education for a fellowship that made possible the initial year of research on this book (1970–1971) and also to the University of Virginia for a grant to continue the research during the summer of 1973. A word of special thanks is due to my friend, M. André Bleikasten, of the English Institute faculty in the University of Strasbourg for first introducing me to structuralism. As always, my wife and sons have been supportive throughout.

DAN OTTO VIA, JR.

University of Virginia
Charlottesville, Virginia
September, 1974

Introduction

The principal objects of my concern in this book are three Pauline texts and the Gospel of Mark. Since the Gospels are narratives, it would not be surprising to find someone using terms drawn from the criticism of drama and fiction in order to interpret them. But is there any reason—other than the desire to be novel and "literary"—for employing the category of comedy as a means of interpreting Paul's kerygma? At the beginning I should like to suggest in a provisional and general way a dual justification for the direction I am about to take, making two points which will be developed more fully as the discussion proceeds: (1) Death and resurrection are the kernel of Paul's kerygma, and the passion narrative obviously looms large in Mark; death and resurrection are also the generative image which lies at the origins of Greek comedy. (2) Certain particular motifs which emerged in comedy as the form developed appear also in Paul, as he unfolds the kerygma theologically, and in the Markan narrative.

The methodology which I am trying to develop in this work places a certain emphasis on structuralism and represents some modification and reorientation of, but not an abandonment of, the "literary-existential" hermeneutic which I was seeking to articulate in my book, *The Parables*. I should say, however, that my more recent reflections do not present a programmatically structuralist approach, but rather attempt to work out a genuinely literary-critical hermeneutic for the New Testament based on a synthesis of structuralist,[1] phenomenological, and existentialist modes of interpretation.[2] I hope that this methodology may also prove fruitful in approaching other parts of the New Testament.

NOTES TO INTRODUCTION

1. For the position that no *one* method can do the whole interpretive task see Robert Champigny, "Structural Analysis and Literary Criticism," p. 3; unpublished paper delivered at the Modern Language Association, New York, December, 1972.

2. For the view that some sort of synthesis of phenomenological and structuralist criticism offers a viable option for American literary criticism see Robert Magliola, "Parisian Structuralism Confronts Phenomenology: The Ongoing Debate," pp. 5, 10; unpublished paper delivered at the Modern Language Association, New York, December, 1972.

A Structuralist-Literary Approach to New Testament Hermeneutic

A. History and Structure: Diachrony and Synchrony

At the outset I should like to give some indication of the nature of structuralism or structural analysis or structuralist activity and to suggest later on how it might prove to be fruitful for the interpretation of the New Testament.

There is a question as to whether structuralism is simply a method of analysis and an activity or is also an "ideology." While structuralism as a method is not tied to any one ideology but is compatible with a number of different ones,[1] it is my judgment that the method inevitably involves some ideological—I would prefer to say "philosophical"—entailments. What these are for me I shall try to make clear as I proceed.

With regard to origins within reasonable limits, structuralism goes back to the structural linguistics of Ferdinand de Saussure, whose insights were given a "poetic" turn by the Russian formalists (1920–1925) and especially by Roman Jakobson. The movement may also owe something to phenomenology, particularly to Merleau-Ponty, but it is primarily the anthropologist, Claude Lévi-Strauss, who made it the intellectual fashion in the Paris of the 1960s. One of the philosophical spinoffs from this was the end of existentialism as the reigning mode of philosophy in Paris, as people began to listen less to Sartre and more to Michel Foucault,[2] who denies that he is a structuralist but is held to be one, more or less, by many others.[3] Now that the period of structuralism's Parisian modishness is past and the movement has become much more widely known out-side of France, it is time for a more circumspect assessment of its value as a method of explanation.

Any adoption and adaptation of structuralism by New Testament hermeneutic will entail, not a rejection of the historical method, but a relegating of it to a more marginal position than it has been en-joying. For many decades the critically orthodox New Testament scholar has asked historical questions, has sought to use a historical methodology, and has expected historical results. The goal has been to understand a New Testament theme by pushing through the em-ployed conceptualizations and traditions to the historical situation from which the theme came and to see that situation within the broad trajectories that were in process in the milieu of early Chris-tianity.[4] Despite this undiluted intention to be historical, the New Testament scholar has been chided from within the theological com-munity for not being historical enough to escape the suspicions of "real" historians.[5]

This overriding concern for history hardly needs to be docu-mented, but two examples may be cited which bear materially on my discussion in the subsequent chapters. It has been argued that early Christianity in its environment had to assume the form of a Hel-lenistic *kurios* cult with the latter's death and resurrection motif.[6] This obviously means that New Testament Christology is a product of the generating power of the environment of early Christianity.[7] On the other hand, it has been denied that the Hellenistic mystery religions influenced Paul's death-resurrection theme, the argument being that the alleged resurrections of Hellenistic deities were noth-ing like the resurrection in the Christian sense, that these resur-rections were not redemptive, or if they were, they took on this character only after New Testament times.[8] I wish neither to deny nor to affirm either Paul's historical dependence upon or indepen-dence of Hellenistic religions. Both of these positions are concerned in their opposite ways with the question whether there is a causal-genetic relationship between the Pauline death-resurrection motif and the environment of early Christianity. I want to pursue an argument later on that this is not the only and not necessarily the most fruitful question to raise with regard to the interpretation of New Testament texts.

It is ironical that this same historical concern has manifested itself so strongly in redaction criticism. The latter discipline represents presumably a turning away from the *process* of oral tradition to a consideration of each (Synoptic) Gospel as a written text expressing the theological motive, purpose, and interpretation of the Evangelist.[9] The irony is that before each Gospel has been looked at in itself it has been turned into a source for its historical *Sitz im Leben*[10] or a product of that *Sitz*,[11] and the theological development from one Gospel to another is taken to be an important piece of evidence for the history of primitive Christianity.[12] Some scholars, in fact, are not even willing to lend the term "redaction-critical" to a study of an Evangelist's theology which does not put at the center the question of the relationship of the Gospel to its *Sitz*.[13]

Is an author to be understood primarily from the structure of his own language or from something else, his environment? Surely the environment cannot be ignored, but to the degree to which it is important, does the environment have to be understood primarily or exclusively as the trajectile movement of the religious-cultural milieu of concepts, images, myths, and practices? Perhaps the environment could be the structure—in the structuralist sense—to which the texts belong, and what is held to be true about New Testament texts must accord with what linguistic and literary scholarship has discovered about the nature of texts as such.[14]

Clearly all structuralists cannot be pressed into the same mold, but, however structuralism is conceived, it comes into some degree of conflict with New Testament scholarship as usually practiced, and this conflict we may begin to penetrate by considering a basic distinction which is made by structuralism, that between synchrony and diachrony. Synchrony refers to the organization, arrangement, and state of a system at a given time and diachrony to the changes and evolutions in the system in the course of time. With regard to language Saussure maintains that synchronic and diachronic studies cannot be pursued simultaneously, and one may find total denials of the intelligibility of diachrony.[15] Roland Barthes states that our distinction suggests some revision of the idea of history since synchrony "accredits a certain immobilization of time."[16]

The import and implications of the distinction between synchrony and diachrony are not easy to grasp, but I think that some light might be shed by recognizing that the distinction is employed within two related but different frames of reference: (1) the phenomena to be analyzed (as, for example, the myths of a given culture), (2) the method of analysis. As for the phenomena themselves, Lévi-Strauss points out that in myth-making societies synchrony and diachrony are in a constant struggle with each other, the effort being to make synchrony dominant, although societies differ on the matter of the intensity of this effort. When the structure or system of a society is challenged, changed, or shattered by a historical event, then the myth-maker, using the *bricoles* or debris from the event, creates a new myth out of this debris. He creates a structure out of the events, and he makes the new structure as much like the old one as possible. The purpose of this effort, conscious or unconscious, is to create a timeless model of reality which will be not merely a stage in the historical process. The fundamental motive is to neutralize history, to undercut diachrony, so as to cushion the society against the shock of change and to remain in synchrony. It is not possible to do this completely: the new does insist on expressing itself. Therefore, the primitive society steers some kind of middle course between change and intelligibility, event and structure, diachrony and synchrony.[17]

Now structuralism as a method of analysis has often been accused of being anti-historical. If much modern scholarship has suffered from an indigestion of history, the cure offered by structuralism is worse than the disease.[18] Such a charge might receive some justification from Barthes's reference to synchrony's "immobilization of time," and I would judge that the work of Michel Foucault does present an excessively anti-historical point of view.

The goal of Foucault's analysis of cultural-intellectual phenomena is to elucidate the principles which are unconsciously assumed by all fields of scholarly knowledge at a given time, the principles which qualify a given discourse as scientific and true. Foucault wants to articulate the orders in which people feel at home, the epistemological field or *episteme* in which knowledge grounds itself, the concepts around which something seeks to constitute itself as knowledge. In this philosopher's view, within a given epoch there is a configuration of principles which embrace all the fields of knowledge and understanding, say, language, biology, and economics, to use three of his favorite examples.[19] This is to say that Foucault's analysis is radically synchronic; it is concerned with the system at a given time.

Foucault concedes that there are some connections between the epistemological configuration or structure of one epoch and its successor,[20] but the configuration in the succeeding period is so different that what was meaningful in one epoch ceases to be in the next. Something like a will or force brings about the change. It is a rupture or breach which is really an inexplicable and enigmatic mutation, at least for our present state of knowledge.[21] Thus for Foucault diachrony as an account of chronological, causal, genetic development is unintelligible.[22]

Other structuralists would contend, however, that the opposition between synchrony and diachrony is largely illusory because change and movement are to be found within the synchronic system[23] (to be discussed at greater length below in terms of "transformations"). Jean Pouillon sees structuralism as a means of bringing to light different wholes or ensembles as variants of each other, and he seems virtually to deny that there is in principle any difference between synchronic and diachronic transformations or variations, for he asserts that the ensembles which are compared may be two alternative solutions to the same problem, two societies which are actually related, or two successive states of the same whole.[24]

Paul Ricoeur grants to structural analysis a certain legitimacy and does not attribute to it a pure and simple opposition between synchrony and diachrony. But he questions whether it is applicable to a society which is different from the myth-making societies described above by Lévi-Strauss.[25] Ricoeur doubts that structural analysis can account for the self-interpretation of a society which does not try to neutralize history by reestablishing its system but which rather "lives by diachrony." Structuralism distorts the textual tradition of a people which intentionally reinterprets and finds new meanings in its traditions in consequence of unexpected, and sometimes shattering, historical events.[26]

The biblical scholar naturally lends a sympathetic ear to Ricoeur's warning, but there is still more to be said. A. J. Greimas suggests that it is more conceivable and less difficult to compare—synchronically—French, Japanese, and Indian feudalism than it is to compare two structural states on the same time line. The description and comparison of static or synchronic structures must be mastered before we can really understand diachronic transformations. In Greimas's view, given two structures (S_1 and S_2) in the same time line, we do not at the present time possess sufficient historical expertise to demonstrate a diachronic transformation or that S_2 is a transformation of S_1 and not vice versa.[27]

I should like to restate Greimas's last position somewhat more moderately, understanding S_1 and S_2 as texts. In the absence of clear evidence external to the texts themselves, it will often be impossible to show which one is a transformation of the other, that is, what is the diachronic or chronological relationship. This whole discussion should suggest to New Testament scholarship that synchronic analysis affords a method for dealing with materials whose chronological-genetic relationships cannot be determined. The very contrast synchronic/diachronic should provoke us to ask whether certain materials which we treat diachronically offer enough evidence to be so treated and whether that is the most illuminating method.

Synchronic analysis, for example, offers a meaningful way of approaching the Synoptic problem, the relationship between Matthew, Mark, and Luke. The three Gospels are enough alike to be regarded as being in the same time line; probably at least one of them was used by the others. There is, however, no reliable external evidence as to which one is the earliest and as to how they used each other. Most New Testament scholars probably still think that Mark was prior and was a source for Matthew and Luke, but certain recent studies[28] show that the matter is not settled. Plausible cases can be made from internal evidence for the priority of both Mark and Matthew, but the arguments often cancel each other out, and some can be turned in either direction. The problem of priority, the question of the diachronic relationship among the Synoptic Gospels, is very difficult if not impossible, I submit, to answer. Therefore, I respectfully suggest that it not be asked—at least for a long time. What is perfectly possible and potentially fruitful is a generic or synchronic comparative analysis of the three Synoptics.

To whatever degree the tendency is actualized in different structuralists, structuralism does tend to immobilize time. Should we not listen to this and pay attention to the suggestion that hermeneutic should be less concerned about the "temporal tissue" of history, for our knowledge of intimacy depends more on our localization in space than on our localization in a chronological-causal-genetic continuum?[29] Perhaps we should be more concerned about our verticality, represented for us in the image of a house, with its foundation planted in the rocks of the earth and its roof pointing toward the sky.[30]

The structuralist method has an affinity with this latter kind of existential concern. What then exactly is the meaning of the word *structure* for structuralism? Our first move should be to say what it does not mean. Biblical scholarship often uses the term *structure* when discussing a text, and those who speak about articulating the structure of a passage have typically meant exhibiting the pattern, texture, arrangement, or sequence of words in the unit. Developing an outline of a text attempts to reproduce the original plan of the author.[31] But according to a definitional essay, structure in the structuralist sense (which is the sense in which I will generally use the term from now on, unless otherwise indicated) is to be distinguished from the internal organization or arrangement of a text, and it is precisely the making of this distinction which differentiates the reality from the appearance of structuralism. Structure properly speaking is the hidden or underlying configuration that can offer some explanation for the more or less visible or obvious pattern in the text.[32] Thus the goal of structuralist analysis or criticism is not to lead the work back to its origins, to reproduce the original plan of the author, but to produce a new knowledge. Structure is applied from outside and is not derived from the book; the book belongs to the structure without containing it. The work's meaning is not found inside it but beside it, at its limits,[33] at the point where the text is joined to its structure.

B. From Linguistics to Criticism: The Construction of the Structure

The structuralist method is not a single one, but is rather in its various manifestations defined by its object.[34] Even those structuralists who deal with the same kind of object—literary texts (fictional or biblical)—cannot be pressed into the same mold. The second generation of structuralist literary critics grants that structuralist literary criticism is still very much in the beginning stages, that it is yet defining and formulating itself, largely out of the work of Lévi-Strauss on myth and out of structural linguistics, going back especially to Ferdinand de Saussure.[35] One of the interesting phenomena in France, and now to a degree elsewhere, is that both "secular" literary critics and biblical scholars are doing structural analyses of biblical narratives, and in both theological and non-theological media.[36]

Before proceeding further, however, we need to say something more about the relationship between literary criticism (interpretation) and linguistics. Tzvetan Todorov denies that criticism (poetics) can be made to submit docilely to linguistics, yet he affirms the dependence of criticism on linguistics in his assertion that the minimal unit of a narrative is the proposition, which is to be constructed on the model of the nuclear propositions of contemporary grammar. Such an approach to interpretation keeps us at the level of syntax, of connecting one formal proposition to another.[37]

Paul Ricoeur—making a direct response actually to Lévi-Strauss rather than to Todorov—charges structuralism with having chosen syntax against semantics. Structuralism has assimilated all thought to the model of primitive thought, and the latter is a form of thought which does not think itself but is unconsciously accommodated to a system of contrasts or binary oppositions which are independent of the thinker or observer. Ricoeur, again, does not believe that structuralism can account for those cases in which a people reinterprets and finds new significance in a tradition which has a surplus of meaning and does not simply want to neutralize history by reestablishing the system. Structuralism cannot explain those phenomena of reinterpretation which even Lévi-Strauss must attribute to *l'esprit humain*. Ricoeur doubts that the principles operative at the level of meaning are identical with those operating, say, at the level of phonology or syntax.[38]

Todorov argues, however, that syntactical matters such as voice and mood have semantic significance. The active voice in the short story creates an ethic of action, while the passive voice in the fairy story causes a world of passion to rule.[39] For Roland Barthes[40] the syntactic level can suggest a larger meaning (semantic) because elements may relate to levels that are "higher" than the story level as well as to elements which come later in the story itself. That is to say, in terms of figure #1 (see page 12), a* has not only a relation of order to b* and e*, later elements in the story, but also a relationship of meaning to a″, a′, and a, correlative elements from other stories or correlative elements from different but parallel and similar sequences in the same story. (Different structural levels and parallel sequences in the same narrative will be given full interpretive attention in Chapter IV).

The same distinction which exists between worked matter and the product of the work exists between language and literature. A work of literature is both language and art; it is the meeting of two determinations.[41] Now how is this intersection of two different activities to be understood and clarified? I find most-illuminating Michael Polanyi's concept of multileveled comprehensive entities. A machine, a biological organism, a language, a speech are all examples of such entities. In a speech we have the levels of voice-words-syntax-sentence-style-the complete text. Each level operates according to a kind of dual control, being governed by its own laws but also having its boundary open to the control of the next higher level. Words placed in a random order would obey the laws of vocabulary but not those of syntax. If the words were rearranged in a proper syntactical order, the laws of vocabulary would not be annulled but a new and higher principle or order would also come to expression. Each higher level relies on the principles of action in the next lower one—there could be no syntax without vocabulary and phonology—but the higher level cannot be derived from, reduced to, or accounted for by the lower.[42] Thus each level in a text is given its meaning by the next higher level. But what is the level beyond the text that gives meaning to the whole text? That is perhaps the principal question that I am pursuing in this chapter.

Drawing ideas from several sources, I shall attempt to work out a structuralist approach to this question that will, it is hoped, be appropriate to the hermeneutical needs of the several New Testament texts with which I am working and which will also have wider applicability. Working from these texts and toward others, I shall try to construct a structure which will be a system of transformations or variations which can contain these and other possible texts, which will disclose the kinds of relationships between the texts, which will not simply be a common denominator, which will be something-other-than the texts themselves onto which they can be projected but a something of which they will seem like realizations, and which therefore will provide a basis for assessing the meaning of the texts.[43] Now how can this sentence be broken down somewhat?

The program of Lévi-Strauss is to discover the hidden structure that *unconsciously* informs the various aspects of a society—economics, marriage customs, law, language, art, myth, ritual, religion, etc. (He concedes that some elements resist structuring.) All of these are to be seen as variations of one system or structure,[44] and Lévi-Strauss's ultimate goal is to discover the very structure of the human mind.[45] It is also noteworthy that Lévi-Strauss emphasizes the great supremacy of structure to content. For him "terms never have any intrinsic significance," but "their meaning is one of 'position.'" As supporting evidence he notes, for example, that the opposition white/red in one society can be replaced in another culture by the opposition black + white/0 without any change of semantic load or meaning, and it must be granted that Lévi-Strauss makes the same claim when discussing word oppositions—a change of words with no change of meaning.[46]

Might we not say, however, that the point is easier to prove if one does employ as evidence colors used in ritual acts rather than words? One may doubt that words are so empty. G. S. Kirk faults Lévi-Strauss both with ignoring important points of content in certain cases and with using points of content in his interpretations in certain other cases, in contradiction with his own (Lévi-Strauss's) stated methodology.[47] To some extent Paul Ricoeur would agree with Lévi-Strauss that a word becomes truly significant only when it is positioned in a sentence. On the other hand, Ricoeur affirms that while the sentence is transitory the word survives it and is always available for new and different employments.[48] I would suggest that it is not words' lack of content but at least partly their polysemous nature that enables them to have different meanings in different positions while it *is* their position in a structure which determines *which* connotation or nuance will come to the fore. What is said here about the relationship of words to sentences would apply in principle to the relationship of elements or operations to a narrative.

As already indicated, my project is far more modest than that of Lévi-Strauss. It is simply to construct a structure which will help to explain some New Testament texts, which would be *one* of the kinds of structures that Lévi-Strauss might include within his super-structures. One begins more or less at random with a text—narrative or otherwise—which affords some presentiment of being a unit. The process of analysis will have to determine whether in fact it is a unit.[49] Then by the systematic use of intuition one thrusts toward the unknown, which is not quite unknown. That is, one seeks gradually to establish intelligible relations between the initial text and other texts, noting common elements which may be quite differently distributed.[50] Thus from these texts is built up a hypothetical model from which one can descend to other texts which both participate in and depart from it.[51] And so the dialectical process goes on.

Although the analyst may choose his beginning text at random, his intention should be, according to Roland Barthes, to describe things only from *one* point of view. Therefore, he develops a corpus of homogeneous materials which is an autonomous system simply because he decides that for the sake of a given analysis there will be but one point of relevance.[52] In Barthes's view the corpus should be homogeneous in time as well as in substance. It ought to eliminate diachronic elements and be a synchronic cross-section of history.[53] However, I will go with other scholars who are prepared to include within a structure and to treat synchronically elements which are widely separated chronologically, or whose historical connections cannot be proved, but which have structural relationships.[54]

Now what does this model or corpus or structure look like? How can it be formalized? The formalization which I have chosen—there could be other ways—is a grid composed of intersecting horizontal and vertical axes. Each horizontal axis is called a syntagm. The syntagm is a linear and irreversible succession or chain of words connected with each other before and after, and it may be spoken or written. It is the text, narrative or semi-narrative, as it stands. Its type is the sentence and the sentence may be regarded as a homologue of the narrative, the latter being a great "sentence." The spectacle itself is constituted by the syntagm, and ordinarily one would begin analysis with the syntagmatic axis.[55]

Each vertical axis is called a paradigm or system. It is composed of operations or elements from the different texts (narratives) which have something in common, some kind of correlation. It is also the reservoir from which each term in the syntagm was chosen. For example, one of the paradigms in Racine's plays is what Barthes has called the erotic scene, in which the birth of love is recalled. Three elements in this paradigm are Nero's reliving of the moment in which he fell in love with Junia (*Britannicus*), Eriphyle's recalling of her seduction by Achilles (*Iphigenie*), and Athaliah's dream (*Athalie*).[56] These three scenes are elements in one of the vertical axes (paradigms) which intersect the plots or horizontal axes (syntagms) of Racine's plays. The term *opposition* has become the customary one for the relationship between the terms in the paradigm, but since the relationship need not be antonymic, "correlation" is perhaps the better term.

To recapitulate, the grid can be composed by paralleling different texts. Thus structural analysis is concerned about the relationship of a text to a (relative) superstructure or genre (see below). This is largely my interest in Chapters I and II. The grid can also be constructed by superposing similar sequences from the same narrative[57] and by paralleling similar sequences from the same text. Thus structuralist criticism is concerned about the relationship of a text to the various substructures or levels within it. This will be my primary interest in Chapter IV. Without any content filled in, structure as I have been discussing it is simply that which is represented in figure #1. The latter is constructed in such a way as to suggest that

FIGURE #1

syntagm——→

narrative #1	a	b	c	d	e
narrative #2	a'		c'	d'	e'
narrative #3	a''	b''		d''	e''
narrative #4	a*	b*			e*

paradigm

each version or transformation or syntagm will not manifest the same degree of development.

Two points which have been touched on in the foregoing discussion, and which cannot be rigidly separated, now call for further treatment.

(1) The first of these is the theme of silence or hiddenness or the unconscious which attaches to the structuralist concept of structure. It may be recalled that for Heidegger the goal of phenomenology is to let something that lies hidden be seen, that hidden something which really constitutes the meaning and ground of the phenomenon.[58] With regard to the interpretation of texts Heidegger stated that a part of its goal is to show—by the use of violence if necessary—what is said in the text but not in its words.[59]

In a similar vein Merleau-Ponty stated that language is not the translation of a prior text but is, at its deepest, silence. That is to say, meaning is not really in the words but in the intervals between them.[60] In response to this one might say that, even if Merleau-Ponty is right, meaning would still not appear without the words to create the intervals; therefore, it is an overstatement to say that language is silence. Merleau-Ponty concedes that language by breaking the silence realizes what silence wanted but did not attain.[61]

When we come to structuralism we find the broad consensus that in the "natural" state of things the structures of the cultural-intellectual world are invisible or unintelligible or unconscious.[62] The culture's ways of thinking are unconsciously there in eloquent silence.[63] Lévi-Strauss claims in his autobiography that he has learned the most from Marx, Freud, and geology: the true reality is never that lying most open to view, but the nature of truth is indicated by the care which it takes to hide itself.[64] An obvious, simple example cited by Lévi-Strauss is that a learned linguist is unconscious of his phonological and grammatical knowledge when he is acting as a speaking agent.[65] If it is recognized with Ricoeur[66] that, despite the reference to Freud, the unconscious which is in mind here is not so much the Freudian unconscious of desire as the Kantian unconscious of the categories through which we think, then structuralism's possible threat to man's conscious freedom is at least mitigated if not eliminated.[67]

In summary, at this point, structure in one sense is the hidden and unconscious system of presuppositions which accounts for and holds together the visible, existing order, including its literary texts.[68]

(2) We may observe that structure in the sense just discussed exists there in (or around) the phenomena, independently of the

theoretician. The theoretician's discovery of the structure will lead to some degree of formalization of it.[69] This formalization, or structure, is an object constructed by the analyst which is an imitation of the original object. It is distinct from but related to the original phenomenon, and its purpose is to make articulately intelligible that which was hidden or unintelligible in the natural object. The structuralist activity involves the fabrication of meaning.[70] With regard to literary criticism in particular, structuralist analysis entails the creation of a "discourse upon discourse," a second or metalanguage to operate upon the language of the text.[71] This metalanguage—this constructed structure—provides a horizon of meaning for conscious hermeneutical work on the text.

C. Ways of Conceiving the Structure

I should now like to discuss several ways of conceiving structure in the second sense—the critical metalanguage with its diagrammatic formalization—which will help to clarify the significance of figure #1.

1. Literary Discourse and Genre

Todorov points out that there are two fundamental attitudes which one may take toward a literary work: (1) one may regard the work itself as an ultimate goal; or (2) one may take it as the manifestation of something else.

With reference to the first view, if anything is said about the work other than repeating it word for word, then the work is inevitably transposed into another discourse, and the ideal has been abandoned. This point of view can regard criticism only as an unfortunate inevitability.

The second point of view consciously seeks to transpose the meaning of the literary work into a type of discourse which is regarded as more fundamental—psychological, sociological, philosophical, etc. Such a procedure is legitimate but is not literary criticism proper—what Todorov calls *poétique*. Poetic does share with the second point of view the projection of the work onto something other than itself, but that other thing is not heterogeneous. It is rather literary discourse itself or *littérarité*—that general abstract structure, that tableau of possibilities, that system of formal properties (plot, causality, point of view, degree of reference to the "real" world, etc.)—which makes the work possible and of which a given work seems to be a realization.[72]

The structure or grid of syntagms and paradigms is what Lévi-Strauss would call a "set" (of myths)[73] and Todorov a "genre." Thus for Todorov there is a close connection between *littérarité* and genre. The genre is constructed by abstracting from several works a number of traits which they have in common (although the traits will appear as variations or transformations of each other) and which are deemed to be more important than other traits which they do not have in common. Todorov finds, for example, that *Tristram Shandy, The Unnamable*, and *Notes from the Underground* (Part I) comprise a genre. The genre is that beyond the text from which the latter draws its meaning.[74] Thus we see that the process of structuralist analysis is both analytical and totalizing; it decomposes and recomposes "on a different plane."[75] The syntagm is broken down so that each element may be related to its paradigm and each element and each syntagm may be viewed against the horizon-perspective which the structure is. The genre-structure, the grid, is the new system in which the syntagm may be reconstructed. In sum, literary discourse is the totality of formal possibilities, while genre represents a certain selection from among these possibilities. This will be further developed in Section C, 3 below.

My purpose, now stated somewhat more concretely and specifically, is to construct a nonconventional version of the comic (or tragicomic) genre-structure into which New Testament texts may be placed and hence better understood.

Let me now make several points by way of summary and prospect: The set, genre, or structure does not have a single "true" or "earlier" version. Rather it is made up of all of its versions or transformations. The relationship between the syntagms is logical, not genetic,[76] and no one syntagm or narrative has a privileged position. The structuralist goal is to render an account of the transformations,[77] and my particular aim is to give an account of the variations among several kerygma-based Pauline texts and the much greater variation between these Pauline passages and the Gospel of Mark by making use of the comic genre-structure.

Behind the narrative (syntagm) there is a logical structure, a superior order (the paradigms, the structure) which to some degree governs the syntagm and is pertinent for its meaning and which has a certain independence of the "before and after" of the narrative.[78]

In establishing a paradigm the analyst's preunderstanding is at work in dialectical relationship with the materials as he decides what elements are to go into the vertical axis. This is where the hermeneutical process comes to the fore, for the interpreter must *discover* what elements belong to the paradigm, which is a matter of *discerning* what they logically have in common rather than depending on the *narrative* order of the texts (syntagm).[79] That is, elements connected in the syntagm may have to be separated in order to show to what paradigm they belong. Thus with regard to our model structure (figure #1) element a, for example, is seen in some sense *as* a′, a″, and a*, and each syntagm is seen in the light of the whole structure-system. Also an element in a narrative which may be quite puzzling, or even inexplicable, at the syntagmatic level, that is, which is not prepared for by any prior element in the story, may become understandable as something which has come into the syntagm from the paradigm (note a concrete case of this in Chapter II).

Seeing the text as a syntagm or transformation within the genre is a way of saying something new about the text and not merely identifying its hidden internal meaning. My adaptation of Todorov's concept of genre places the text in relation to its limit, in relation to that other (the genre) from which it came, an other which is external to the text itself. This kind of interpretation is innovative hopefully because judgment must be used in deciding which traits create the genre, and the genre casts light on the text. At the same time the genre-model-structure is a gestalt which owes something to, is constructed from, a number of texts—including the one to be interpreted—which are deemed to be in some way akin; there is a dialectical relationship between the text and the structure-system. By proceeding in this way we can avoid arbitrariness, or eisegesis.

It is permissible to use the fullest syntagm as a key in setting up the structure as long as the less complete versions are distinguished from the most complete only by omissions. If there are *differences,* however, in treating the same episode, then the transformation must be accounted for.[80]

Let us observe several of the kinds of transformations which may occur. They pertain especially to myth, but some of them could occur equally well in other types of narratives: (1) An element in one myth becomes its opposite in another. For example, a myth about wind and water may really be about the origin of fire and be a transformation of another myth which speaks explicitly about the origin of fire. Wind and water are anti-fire, the opposite of fire. (2) We may find mutations in characters and relationships and inversions of relationships.[81] (3) Transformations may be brought about by devices such as putting old terms in new contexts[82] or simply by altering the voice of the verbs (explicitly or implicitly), which is sufficient, for example, to turn a fairy story (passive) into a short story (active).[83] We may also find the *insertion* or *deletion* of a grammatically possible unit, or the *substitution* of one such element for another (including the subtypes of substitution, *expansion* and *reduction*), or a *permutation,* which involves removing an element from one place in a syntagm and hooking it in at another syntactically possible place.[84]

For Lévi-Strauss[85] the dynamic behind transformation is that two opposite terms which have no intermediary tend to be replaced by two equivalent terms which do admit a mediator.

Initial Pair   *First Triad*
Life

                                        Agriculture
                                        Hunting
                                        Warfare

Death

Ultimately for Lévi-Strauss this process is grounded in the fundamental structure of the human mind, which comprehends both primitive and modern thought, and which seeks to organize the universe "as a continuum made up of successive oppositions."[86] For my part, I would like to leave in suspense, at least for the time being, the question of the structure of the human mind and to affirm my belief that historical, cultural, and conceptual factors must be taken into account when trying to explain transformations within a set or a structure, a point Lévi-Strauss[87] would agree to within limits.

2. Signifier and Signified

Linguistics, especially in its semantic aspects, makes considerable use of the concept of the *sign,* the stimulus to which we respond when we think,[88] or that with which we think. The sign is constituted by the unity of two aspects, the signifier and the signified, which cannot be separated in human language. The signifier belongs to the plane of expression and the external. It is the mediator, the bearer of meaning; and something material is always necessary to it —sounds, objects, or images. The signified belongs to the plane of content and the internal. For Saussure the signified was the mental image of a thing represented by a word. The signified of the sign "ox" is not the animal but the mental image of it. In Barthes's view, however, this position smacks too much of psychologism. The signified can be defined only tautologically (within the signifying process which combines signifier and signified in the sign) as the "something . . . meant by the person who uses the sign."[89]

The hermeneutical circle is grounded in the fundamental signifying process in which signifier and signified react on each other. Statements mean different things to different people and literary works change their meanings from period to period, not merely because of misunderstanding on the part of the interpreter but because of the fact that the signified is both a product of the objective structure of the signifier and is also the subjective structure of preunderstanding with which the individual apprehends the signifier.[90]

Paul Ricoeur accuses structuralism, however, of detaching the analyst from any involvement in the object of his study and of trying to deny the hermeneutical circle.[91] Is this true of all structuralists? Roland Barthes (who is a structuralist critic among other things) uses the opposition signifier/signified both to define the nature of the literary text and also to describe the activity of criticism.

With regard to the nature of the literary text Barthes observes that a work of literature was long thought of—and still is by "university" or "academic" critics—as the product of a cause. It has a causal-genetic relationship with something other than itself. The work is a product growing out of a source, whether that source be considered to be an antecedent work, a biographical circumstance, or some "passion" experienced by the author.[92] In Barthes's opinion this view of the text leads to dealing with only a small part of it or to trying to establish relationships that are impossible to maintain. Therefore, the idea of the work as a product gave way to that of a sign. The work would be a sign of something beyond itself.[93]

This view of the text means that criticism is to consist not in treating the work as the effect of a cause but in opening it up as the signifier of a signified.[94] Now what is the relationship between these two factors? At one point Barthes suggests, if he does not assert, that one should begin with an immanent or internal analysis of the work (signifier) itself and only after that should one posit its relation to the world—that is, to its signified, the world understood in a certain way. He can also say that this internal analysis does not entail the discovery of some hidden secret.[95] In any case the signifier is more-or-less available while the signified is what must be discovered. One moves from signifier to signified.[96]

When Barthes speaks this way he may be considering only half of the hermeneutical circle in isolation from the other half. On the other hand, he may be rejecting the hermeneutical circle and adopting a nonphenomenological position (the phenomenological rejection of the subject/object dichotomy supports the hermeneutical circle). Yet in other passages he seems to work with a phenomenological perspective and to take full cognizance of the hermeneutical circle. And this, I must confess, is the Barthes which I find most helpful.[97] He can say that the goal of criticism *is* to discover the signifier's hidden signified[98] and also suggest that one cannot ascertain the signifier without first positing the signified.[99] Therefore, the signified is both the preunderstanding from which one approaches the text and the new understanding which results from an encounter with it, or it is the line connecting these two aspects.

For every signifier there are always several possible signifieds. One cannot "tell the truth" about Racine, for example, for he can be read in several different languages—psychoanalytical, existential, tragic, etc. One must immerse oneself in Racine and then take the risk of talking about Racine in one way and not in another. The choice of a signified—the level of the world at which the text is to be understood (existential, psychological, or what have you)—is never innocent or neutral but reveals the situation of the critic.[100] In his analysis of Racine, Barthes's signified for the signifiers—the Racine plays—is both psychoanalytical and theological. That is, the destiny against which the tragic hero struggles is the Freudian primal father and the Old Testament God of the Jews.[101] The first objective rule of interpretation, then, is to declare the "system of reading" from which one will approach the text. In Barthes's view the effort to keep the signified at the most factual level is not so much a function of objectivity as of timidity and banality, and its result is to cut off interpretation at the point at which it is likely to become enlightening.[102]

A simple biblical example of the interaction of signifier and signified is the obvious fact that Old Testament texts (signifiers) appear in the New Testament (the context for a new signified). This produces a polyvalent signification and shows that the original (Old Testament) text did not have a closed signification.[103]

Even Lévi-Strauss in his own way has a hermeneutical circle because for him the human mind generates myths as images of the world, and the mind is in the end the signified to which they refer.[104] But this does not overcome Ricoeur's charge that Lévi-Strauss's structuralism, at least, disengages the analyst, or even the nonreflective thinker, from personal involvement in his understanding of existence. For Lévi-Strauss the fundamental condition for the existence of thought is "an objective structure of the psyche and brain" which organizes the world as a universe of oppositions.[105]

During the 1960s in Paris a battle raged between the structuralist critics, with Barthes taking the lead for the structuralists, and the so-called university critics, who were represented, among others, by the distinguished Raymond Picard.

Picard charged that structuralist criticism—without even realizing it—oscillates between two views of the literary work. On the one hand, the work is seen as having a fixed, internal structure and meaning, while, on the other hand, it is viewed as a kind of Rorschach image which has no meaning of its own but only the meaning which each age gives it. The structuralist wants to make the work a mere possibility brought to life by the reader's subjectivity.[106] It is the second of these two positions that Picard objects to and that he really identifies structuralism with. Picard himself calls for a flexible, humanistic, but objective neopositivism in criticism which will see the work as built on a solidity of language that will afford objective explications. For Picard the most important level in Racine seems to be the literal meaning of his words, which was obligatory for the seventeenth-century audience and which cannot be ignored.[107] By "literal" Picard seems to mean a referential pointing to something in the seventeenth-century context.

A critic *should* decide whether he is going to view a work *primarily* as a fixed structure of meaning or a kind of polyvalent opening to a number of possible signifieds. But is the distinction between these two as hard and fast as Picard seems to suggest? Let us grant that it is possible to determine with some degree of success and objectivity what an author consciously intends to say, that is, what he means.[108] It is still true that an author never attends in the same degree to or is equally conscious of all aspects of his meaning;[109] moreover, as Elizabeth Sewell points out, language surpasses an author's own powers of exegesis, and it is the nature of language and mind together to generate new meanings.[110] Thus even if a work contains a kind of objective core of meaning, it is still open to various kinds of signifieds. In implicitly rejecting the hermeneutical circle Picard simply ignores what phenomenology has done to break down the subject/object dichotomy and to illuminate the constitutive role of the subject in perception.[111] By staying close to the texts themselves I have tried to protect the concept of genre from the charge of undue subjectivity.

The hermeneutical circle involves the interpretation of the interpreter, which suggests the concept of language event—the interpreter is engaged. The "new hermeneutic" has usually discussed the language event from the standpoint of the power of the text to strike home in the heart because of its manifest content of meaning or because of the power of the unity of form and content. But the possibility of language event can be grounded more fundamentally in the very signifying capacity of language as such. This capacity will be discussed in connection with the symbol, but it also holds true for "lower" forms of signs, which are included in the symbol.

Paul Ricoeur shows that three dualities constitute the symbol: (1) that of signifier (s-p-o-t) and signified ("spot") in the sign, (2) that between the sign and the thing designated (something dirty on something else). To these two dualities which relate to every sign the symbol adds a third: that between the thing designated and another and different meaning, a something else which both gives and hides itself in the immediate sense (man's "uncleanness" before the transcendent).[112] The literal meaning "spot" or "stain" has a further intentionality which it reveals and conceals, a certain situation vis-à-vis the sacred—man's defilement. In the Old Testament defilement is something real and positive although it is like an external infection. Sin, on the other hand, is internal, is the breach of a prior personal bond with God and is, therefore, a lack or a nothingness. When defilement and sin are combined, defilement contributes to sin (lack) a positive quality and makes sin the power which binds man.[113] We might say, then, that a symbol contains a certain semantic space or distance between the literal meaning and the suggested (symbolic) meaning. Signification is the act or process of moving across that space from one level of meaning to another.[114] Thus in these terms the language event is my being carried along by the movement of the signifying process from the literal to the symbolic meaning and my being assimilated to and made a participant in the reality which is symbolized.[115] We should remind ourselves that this is as true for the speaker as for the hearer.[116]

3. Text and Gattung

I turn now to a New Testament scholar's significant contribution to the methodological discussion. Erhardt Güttgemanns intends to develop a New Testament theology—which he calls "generative poetic"—not just in relation to but based upon linguistic-literary methods.[117] This move involves the supersession of both the historical-critical and the existentialist-hermeneutical elements in current New Testament theology. Yet theology is to remain the science of the speech of (Rede von) God or the science of texts about God. The pragmatic goal of such a scientific theology is the methodological penetration of the speech of God, not the existential execution of the latter.[118]

In the service of this effort Güttgemanns develops a concept of text and Gattung (genre) based on "text-linguistics," the meaning of which is now to be discussed. Fundamental to his approach is the affirmation that language occurs only as texts and texts can be classified according to Gattungen. Texts appear as special ways of expression and formation.[119] Following the American linguists

Harris and Chomsky, Güttgemanns makes a basic distinction between performance and competence texts. The former are texts which the competent speaker/hearer has actually realized out of the repertoire of possibilities. The texts of the Bible and texts about them in the history of interpretation are performance texts. Competence texts are those which the competent speaker/hearer has not yet actualized from his repertoire of possibilities but *can* generate at any time from his language-competence.[120] Thus there are apparently three magnitudes in view: (1) texts (performance and competence), (2) Gattungen, (3) and language-competence. Two crucial questions present themselves for theological reflection: (1) In what relationship do the performance texts in the Bible and the interpretive tradition stand to the as yet unrealized competence texts of later interpretation? (2) From what speech-competence are the texts and Gattungen generated and varied?[121] These questions are pursued here in reverse order.

I used the term *apparently* in mentioning three magnitudes because Güttgemanns sometimes seems to distinguish Gattung from speech-competence, while at other times the distinction is not clear. In any case it would appear that speech-competence is a kind of super-genre which determines Gattungen while a Gattung is a genre which constitutes texts in a certain way and thereby classifies them. Thus I think that I will not misrepresent Güttgemanns's basic position if I simply discuss text and Gattung in their interrelationship.

According to Güttgemanns, New Testament theology, as generative poetic, has to do exclusively with its sole given: texts in their linguisticality, and not with an alleged nonlinguistic history which lies behind the texts. Texts are not generated by socio-historical factors. Meaning or semantic effect is not determined by the additive aggregation of units (as tradition plus redaction) to form a text. Neither is meaning constituted by the aggregation of ideas in historical sequence, for example, the development of christological formulas and hymns as Christianity moved from one cultural milieu to another.[122]

A text is a structure which comprises several linguistic levels or dimensions: phonemes (sound), morphemes (form), lexemes (words), textemes (larger units of meaning both syntagmatic and paradigmatic), etc. Semantic effect depends on the interplay of these levels.[123] Let me note here that, when I later attempt to define my approach to the Gospel of Mark, I will translate these linguistic levels (factors of language) by analogy into literary levels (factors of narrative), and will indicate the significance of the interplay of levels.

Despite Güttgemanns's emphasis on the exclusively linguistic object of New Testament theology, he regards the text as the correlation between sender, receiver, subject matter, and circumstances in a functional field. The sender wants to communicate with the receiver through a text. The text is the means of communication which forms a unity with its channel (sound, writing, printing) which in its turn is encoded as a language system (code). Sender and receiver must share the same code and context (verbal and nonverbal situational elements).[124]

These elements in the communication field can be correlated to the six primary speech functions: (1) The expressive function is oriented to the inwardness of the sender. (2) The conative function seeks to affect the receiver. (3) The referential function is coordinated to the context. (4) The "phatic" function tests whether the channel is working by, say, simply starting or cutting off communication. (5) The metalinguistic function is concerned with whether the code is working understandably. (6) The poetic function focuses on the text for its own sake.[125]

Now if texts are not generated by history, neither are they generated by other performance texts. The competence which generates them is rather grammar or syntax, not grammar in the traditional sense but modern transformational grammar which classifies texts. Such a grammar is a matrix of meaning, a repertoire of possibilities, a system of generative forces which procreates texts.[126] For Güttgemanns Gattung is a synonym or functional equivalent of grammar. Therefore Gattung is the competence which generates a text as one form of expression and not as another: it orders the linguistic levels (textemes, etc.) and the elements which compose them by selection and arrangement, and it also establishes the relative dominance or hierarchy of the speech functions by selection and combination. Thus in the Gattung parable the poetic function predominates while in theological discourse the metalinguistic (not referential) function is dominant.[127]

If one asks what the ultimate locus of Gattung is, I am not sure what Güttgemanns would say. But, at least as a working hypothesis, I will take my cue from Chomsky. His view (admittedly rationalistic) is that certain deep structures are intrinsic to and implicit in the human mind universally and that performance texts are produced from these by various transformations.[128] May we not then say that Gattungen or genres are inherent structures of the human mind,[129] of which there may be an indeterminate number, and that they may be conceptually articulated by analysis?

Güttgemanns goes a step beyond what has already been discussed in that he denies, not only that linguistic texts are generated by history, but that history is generated by history. He does not doubt that there is such a thing as diachronic succession. He would not reject Käsemann's statement that the historical process is composed of changes of direction, setbacks, breakthroughs, and new beginnings.[130] But Güttgemanns does deny that history is an ontologically prior category. It is a mistake to suppose that chronological succession—of traditions or events—is governed by the logic of history rather than by the logic of grammar. The historical process as meaningful, the performance of significative human acts, is ontologically based on the same grammatical matrix which generates linguistic texts.[131]

Güttgemanns provides a critique of Bultmann's existentialist hermeneutic. His global charge is that Bultmann lacks a theory of texts. The semantic load of Bultmann's existentialist universals, through which he intends to translate the language of the New Testament into the language of today, is carried almost exclusively by lexemes (words)—body, heart, flesh, faith, world, freedom, light, darkness, etc. A proper hermeneutic would ask about the relation of the existentials to the multilayeredness of the text and to the matrix which generated it. Existentials should be related to textemes, for example, to the *structure* of the parables.[132]

Güttgemanns continues: there will be no translation unless the textemes of the original language and the goal language function isomorphically. Therefore, we must clarify the linguistic universals which provide the isomorphic factors uniting all languages.[133]

Güttgemanns maintains that the movement from the biblical performance texts to our competence texts belongs to the language-learning theory of transformational grammar and that this movement can be methodologically controlled.[134] Güttgemanns may well be right if our competence texts are texts of theological reflection. But when he explicitly includes preaching as well,[135] I am inclined to demur. One might even describe in terms of transformational grammar how a sermon which has already been preached derived from a given biblical text, but one could hardly control the movement in advance; that is, one could not by the use of scholarly methodology make a contemplated sermon into preaching in the New Testament sense—the happening of the word of God.

Güttgemanns's position becomes more problematical when he carries its logic to the point of suggesting that since the word of God is bound to linguistic texts and is truly *word*—with which I agree— then it can be grasped and traced out by text-linguistics.[136] I would say that the texts can be grasped by text linguistics, but surely no methodology can grasp the word of God *as* word of God. Güttgemanns implies that to oppose his position is to turn the kerygma into referential statements: they refer to something other than themselves.[137] I would respond that some of them in fact do, but even in the case of Jesus' parables or in other kerygmatic statements where the referential function is absent or very slightly at work, the word of God cannot be completely identified with the texts. For the parables and the church's kerygma have a strong conative function. Kerygma is not word of God without a hearer. But there is still more to be said.

The question, again, is whether a biblical text can be translated into another genuinely kerygmatic text exclusively under the control of a linguistic methodology. It is not a matter of wanting to find a nonlinguistic meaning for the word of God which is detachable from or somehow behind the meaning of the text. It is rather the question whether the new (translated) text *as kerygmatic* (language event) can be accounted for exclusively in linguistic terms.

Edgar Haulotte points out that Scripture opens up the possibility of later readings or usages (interpretations) which may be to Scripture as *parole* (the particular word of an individual) to *langue* (his inherited language with its given structure). He, like Güttgemanns, is concerned with the structure—which he also calls a syntax— which can sustain the whole of Scripture, along with its individual parts, and enable it to unfold itself in the readings of the interpretive tradition.[138] For Haulotte the meaning of the word of God does not depart from the text, but it is not simply identical with it. The new text is kerygma or *parole* when a *trans*-linguistic subject is manifested in the linguistic discourse itself. That trans-linguistic subject is the *parole* of God, the reality of God, objectivizing itself in the proper constitution of man.[139] Thus word of God occurs where language changes man's existence. There is interaction between linguistic reality and a reality which cannot without remainder be limited to language. Güttgemanns seems to have something of this in mind when he speaks of the role of the text in the functional field of communication, but this strain in his thought has not been coordinated with his assertions about the exclusive role of language and linguistic methodology.

4. Tacit Knowledge and Problem-Solving

Todorov's genre, Barthes's signified, and Güttgemanns's Gattung correspond functionally to what Michael Polanyi would call a whole, a comprehensive entity, or a universal class concept.[140] Each of these more-or-less synonymous terms may be understood as the answer to a problem, an answer which is at first hidden and which is analogous to what we have been calling structure.

According to Polanyi's theory of tacit knowledge, all knowing is an integration of subsidiary and focal awareness.[141] To know something subsidiarily is to attend from or through that object to a second entity, the latter being that which we know focally.[142] To use Polanyi's terms for the question of interpretation with which we are concerned: the text (or texts) standing alone is a problem because it lacks meaning. The answer, the meaning of the text, would be the articulation of the comprehensive entity to which the text belongs. At the beginning of the process of problem-solving a person is subsidiarily aware of his presuppositions because they are the intellectual tools with which he grasps the world. They are assimilated to his body just as a hammer is; thus he attends from these presuppositions to something else; he has subsidiary knowledge of them just as he has of his body.[143] At this beginning stage the interpreter is focally aware of the text, but in order to understand it, solve the problem of its meaning, he must fuse it into the subsidiary awareness of his presuppositions, and using text and preunderstanding as clues he must shift his focal attention to a gap, an emptiness which is at first not filled in, but behind which he senses and anticipates the presence of a yet hidden knowledge.[144] He shifts his attention back and forth between the subsidiary clues (text, preunderstanding, other possibly related texts) and the gap, until there emerges from behind the gap an articulated elucidation of the comprehensive entity to which the text belongs.[145] The text is properly understood, in Polanyi's view, when one knows it subsidiarily, looks from and through it—and thereby interiorizes it—to the class concept or totality to which it belongs.[146] I would want to add only that Polanyi is here describing the critical stance. For the aesthetic stance, one would shift one's focal attention back to the text.

As a summary for section C: The grid of syntagms and paradigms as described in section B is to be understood as explicated by Todorov's genre, Barthes's signified, and Güttgemanns's Gattung (genre). I do not mean to suggest that genre is the exact equivalent of Barthes's signified but that both function in the same way in relation to the text. Also the chosen signified will undoubtedly influence the construction of the genre-structure. It is at least a part of its logos. That is, the logos of the text is kin to the logos of the genre. This is suggested by Barthes's own statement that either a narrative is insignificant or it possesses *in common with* other narratives a structure accessible to analysis.[147] Working a posteriori the genre is constructed from existing syntagms or performance texts, but the a priori assumption is that the texts were generated by the genre. Both genre and signified are, in Polanyi's terms, the answer to a problem, the problem being to define the level or horizon beyond the texts as a whole (the Pauline passages, the Gospel of Mark) from which the texts derive their meaning.

D. Literary Form-and-Content versus Structural Analysis

It is a revered doctrine of much literary criticism, especially what has long been called in America "new criticism," that the literary work is a centripetally cohering organic unity of form and content. The form is not a container for the content but is rather the arrangement and patterning of it. Meaning depends as much on form as on content. Change the order and you change the meaning. Thus the task of criticism is to clarify what the formal patterns are.

Is any sort of rapprochement possible between this position and structuralist criticism, which manifestly sets out to decompose the work in order to recompose it on another level? Keep in mind that the structural analyst's recomposition is based on his judgment about the (unconscious) structure that controlled the material in the first place. It may be true that form and content cannot be separated in a narrative itself, but they can be for the sake of analysis.

G. S. Kirk maintains that myths do have a content which cannot be ignored and that content changes in the course of retelling a myth, carrying along with it a change of meaning. Structure is not the sole determiner of meaning.[148] (Recall that for Lévi-Strauss mythological thinking is the homologue of all thinking.) In Kirk's opinion, changes may be produced not just by unconscious factors, but also by the tendencies of oral narration or by some particular interest on the part of the storyteller,[149] and we might add, by some particular audience situation. Furthermore, Kirk holds that a change in content entails a change of structure and maintains that his view is based on empirical observations of folk literature, while Lévi-Strauss's view that structure does not change—or changes very little—is derived from his assumption that the structure of all myth is unconscious and is identical with the structure of the human mind.[150]

Now we can hardly ignore Kirk's empirical evidence, but in this day after Freud, Marx, and Nietzsche have taught us in their various ways that consciousness is not the home of meaning[151] we cannot neglect the role of the unconscious. The very fact that—or to the extent that—the myth-maker's (or thinker's) structures of thought are unconscious would mean that his new content would tend to be arranged according to the old structures. Just because the structuring process is to some degree unconscious and the storyteller "feels" free to use his content as he chooses, the materials would tend to be arranged in the same old structure.

Francis Cornford gives some support to this position on the relationship of "freedom" to the unconscious. He points out that the plot of Greek tragedy was primarily *myth* and was bound by the epic tradition. On the other hand, Attic comedy had much freedom in plot development. Its plot was primarily *logos*—the free illustration of a theme with incidents. This very freedom to employ the incidents left standing the old ritual structure from which both comedy and tragedy emerged. The old structure is discernible in comedy but hardly in tragedy.[152] Cornford is implying that the very freedom with which the materials were employed in comedy along with the unconscious assumption of the old ritual pattern gave the latter an opening to manifest itself.

Must we then not posit a reciprocal interaction between the free employment of content and unconscious structuring? Perhaps we should accept Kirk's view as a working hypothesis and Lévi-Strauss's as a limiting concept. That is, the structure of the mind may be a kind of limiting horizon, affecting the kind and number of changes which can take place in human thought, but the possibilities for change are indeterminate and the structure of the human mind is not yet discovered, if it is discoverable.

Now with regard to form I will restrict myself largely but not exclusively to the matter of time as an ordering principle. One may argue that myth lacks any real chronology, for beginning and end are to be apprehended simultaneously, and significance is in the relationships among the component parts. The sequence really is only a constant rearrangement of these parts all of which are present from the start.[153] Speaking of narrative more generally, we can assert that the succession of events in a narrative is dependent on a logical order, and one could interchange the parts of the narrative without affecting the logic.[154]

But is this true of all myth, or all narrative? Paul Ricoeur suggests that one of the achievements of myth, as it expands symbol into narrative, is to introduce into the symbolic discourse, temporality—a before and an after—as a matter for reflection.[155]

But whatever may be true, or seem to be true, of the narratives themselves—even if temporality appears to be important there— Barthes maintains that behind the time of the narrative there is a nontemporal logic. Claiming the support of Aristotle, Greimas, Bremond, and Todorov, and quoting Lévi-Strauss, Barthes states that the chronological succession of a narrative is resorbed into a nontemporal structural matrix. Therefore, the task of critical analysis is to "dechronologize" the narrative and "relogify" it. What the interpreter must do is give a structural description of the chronological illusion.[156]

One would expect a critic still minimally influenced by American new criticism to protest against this approach, and other French critics also oppose it. Raymond Picard objects to the breaking down and dissolving of the literary form, structure, or architecture in order to find a hidden logical structure. He opposes the shattering of the framework of each literary piece in order to establish the lines between different works. The unconscious of the author ought not to be turned into an alibi for the critic to build psychological, sociological, or metaphysical structures in place of literary ones.[157]

One might argue that since the deep, logical structure of a sentence is more fundamental than its surface, grammatical structure,[158] so the logical structure of a narrative is more determinative than its literary form. But recall Polanyi's concept of the nature of multileveled comprehensive entities. What is true at the level of the sentence may not be true for the text as a whole. But then again it might be. The principles governing the higher level transcend but do not annul those governing the lower level.

One is loath to relinquish the organic integrity of the form of the individual work, and the theological analogue of this hesitation is that one is reluctant to surrender the biblical affirmation of the temporality of human existence. At the same time the claims and achievements of structuralism cannot be ignored. Actually Güttgemanns's discussion shows that historical process and temporality need not be incompatible with structural analysis. A further attempt to relate them concretely will be made below in connection with a particular question of Markan interpretation.

NOTES TO CHAPTER I

1. See Günther Schiwy, *Neue Aspekte des Strukturalismus* (München: Kösel Verlag, 1971), pp. 56, 183–187.

2. See Roland Barthes, "L'Analyse Structurale du Récit." *Recherches de Science Religieuse* 58 (January–March, 1970): 17–18; Tzvetan Todorov, "Poétique," *Qu'est-ce que le structuralisme?* ed. François Wahl (Paris: Editions du Seuil, 1968), pp. 106–107, 161; Schiwy, *Neue Aspekte*, pp. 42, 56, 58, 135.

3. See, for example, *Qu'est-ce que le structuralisme*; Jean Piaget, *Structuralism*, trans. C. Maschler (New York: Basic Books, 1970); Schiwy, *Neue Aspekte*, p. 58.

4. See James M. Robinson, "Kerygma and History in the New Testament," *The Bible in Modern Scholarship*, ed. J. P. Hyatt (Nashville and New York: Abingdon, 1965), pp. 149–150; "Introduction: The Dismantling and Reassembling of the Categories of New Testament Scholarship," in James M. Robinson and Helmut Koester, *Trajectories through Early Christianity* (Philadelphia: Fortress Press, 1971), pp. 12–13, 16–17.

5. See Van A. Harvey, *The Historian and the Believer* (Toronto: Macmillan, 1969; paperback edition), pp. 70, 71, 74, 87, 107, 111, 112, 117, 119, 131, 138, 188–189, 249.

6. Wilhelm Bousset, *Kyrios Christos*, trans. J. E. Steely (Nashville: Abingdon Press, 1970), pp. 137, 146, 151, 157.

7. See Hendrikus Boers, "Jesus and the Christian Faith: New Testament Christology since Bousset's *Kyrios Christos*," *Journal of Biblical Literature* 89, part 4 (1970): 453–454, 456.

8. Günther Wagner, *Pauline Baptism and Pagan Mysteries*, trans. J. P. Smith (Edinburgh and London: Oliver and Boyd, 1967), pp. 180–181, 187–195, 198–201, 122–126, 218–221, 268.

9. See Joachim Rodhe, *Rediscovering the Teaching of the Evangelists*, trans. D. M. Barton (Philadelphia: Westminster Press, 1968), pp. 14–20; Norman Perrin, *What is Redaction Criticism?* (Philadelphia: Fortress Press, 1969), pp. 1, 26, 42.

10. Rohde, *Rediscovering*, pp. 19, 22.

11. See Norman Perrin, "The Christology of Mark: A Study in Methodology" in *A Modern Pilgrimage in New Testament Christology* (Philadelphia: Fortress Press, 1974), chap. VIII.

12. Rohde, *Rediscovering*, p. 23.

13. Ibid., pp. 39, 44, 52–53, 72–73. Rohde modifies this position somewhat on pp. 139–140. The same concern to connect a Gospel closely with its historical point of origin and to make the latter the clue to its meaning is seen in J. Louis Martyn, *History and Theology in the Fourth Gospel* (New York: Harper & Row, 1968), p. xvii.

14. See Erhardt Güttgemanns, "Theologie als Sprachbezogene Wissenschaft," *Studia Linguistica Neotestamentica* (München: Christian Kaiser Verlag, 1971), pp. 191–192, 194.

15. See Schiwy, *Neue Aspekte*, p. 37; Paul Ricoeur, "Structure et herméneutique," *Esprit* (nouvelle série), no. 322 (November, 1963): 598–599;

Ricoeur, "La structure, le mot, l'événement," *Esprit* (nouvelle série), no. 360 (May, 1967): 803–804.

16. Roland Barthes, *Critical Essays,* trans. R. Howard (Evanston: Northwestern University Press, 1972), pp. 213–214.

17. See Claude Lévi-Strauss, *The Savage Mind* (Chicago: University of Chicago Press, 1970), pp. 21–22, 26, 68–70, 73–74, 79–81, 155, 197, 231–236.

18. J.-M. Domenach, "Le système et la personne," *Esprit* (nouvelle série), no. 360 (May, 1967): 773–774.

19. Michel Foucault, *The Order of Things,* trans. not indicated (New York: Random House, Pantheon Books, 1970), pp. xi, xiv, xx, xxii, 356, xxiii, 200, 208–209.

20. Ibid., p. 50.

21. Ibid., pp. 166–168, 209, 217, 221, 386.

22. See Pierre Burgelin, "L'archéologie du savior," *Esprit* (nouvelle série), no. 360 (May, 1967): 857.

23. Claude Lévi-Strauss, *Structural Anthropology,* trans. C. Jacobson and B. G. Schoepf (New York: Doubleday, 1967), p. 88; see also Schiwy, *Neue Aspekte,* p. 19.

24. Jean Pouillon, "Présentation: Un Essai de Définition," *Les Temps Modernes* 22, no. 246 (November, 1966): 783.

25. Ricoeur, "Structure," pp. 599, 614.

26. Ricoeur, 'Structure," pp. 599, 612–615; Schiwy, *Neue Aspekte,* p. 59.

27. A. J. Greimas, "Structure et Histoire," *Les Temps Modernes* 22, no. 246 (November, 1966): 824–827.

28. See, for example, William Farmer, *The Synoptic Problem* (New York: Macmillan, 1964); David Dungan, "Mark—The Abridgement of Matthew and Luke," *Jesus and Man's Hope,* I (Pittsburgh: Pittsburgh Theological Seminary, 1970), pp. 51–97.

29. Gaston Bachelard, *The Poetics of Space,* trans. M. Jolas (New York: Orion Press, 1964), p. 9.

30. See ibid., pp. 20, 22, 25.

31. See James Muilenburg, "Form Criticism and Beyond," *Journal of Biblical Literature* 88, part 1 (1969): 8, 17–18; David Greenwood, "Rhetorical Criticism and Formgeschichte: Some Methodological Considerations," *Journal of Biblical Literature* 89, part 4 (1970): 418, 421, 425. The same understanding of the term *structure* is also seen in the usage of the term in Perrin, *Redaction Criticism,* pp. 41 ff.; Charles H. Talbert, "A Non-Pauline Fragment at Romans 3:24–26?" *Journal of Biblical Literature* 85, part 3 (1966): 289 ff.

32. Jean Pouillon, *Présentation,* pp. 774, 776, 779.

33. See Pierre Machery, "L'Analyse littéraire, tombeau des structures," *Les Temps Modernes,* no. 246 (November, 1966): 921–923, 926–928.

34. François Wahl, "Introduction," *Qu 'est-ce que le structuralisme?* p. 8.

35. See Tzvetan Todorov, "Poétique," pp. 106–107, 161.

36. See, for example, *Recherches de Science Religieuse* 58, no. 1 (1970); *Langages* 6, no. 22 (June, 1971); *European Journal of Sociology* 7, no. 1 (1966).

37. Todorov, "Poétique," pp. 107, 133, 139.

38. Ricoeur, "Structure," pp. 604–621.

39. Todorov, "Poétique," pp. 108, 114, 140–142, 147; "Les catégories du récit littéraire," *Communications* 8 (1966): 126, 138.
40. Roland Barthes, "Introduction à l'analyse structurale des récits," *Communications* 8 (1966): 8–9.
41. See Machery, "L'Analyse littéraire," 907–909.
42. Michael Polanyi, *Knowing and Being* (Chicago: University of Chicago Press, 1969), pp. 154–155, 217–218, 227, 237–238. See also Barthes, "Introduction," pp. 3–5.
43. See Todorov, "Poétique," pp. 101–102; André Martinet, "Structure and Language," *Structuralism, Yale French Studies* 36 and 37 (1966): 10–14.
44. Lévi-Strauss, *Anthropology*, pp. 19, 32, 55, 57–58, 61, 64, 82–85, 87, 273–275, 306; *Savage*, pp. 6, 32, 252.
45. Lévi-Strauss, *The Raw and the Cooked*, trans. J. and D. Weightman (New York and Evanston: Harper & Row, Torchbooks, 1970), pp. 10–13, 341; *Savage*, pp. 263–264, 267–268.
46. *Savage*, pp. 53, 55, 64–65, 149–150.
47. G. S. Kirk, *Myth* (Cambridge: Cambridge University Press; Berkeley and Los Angeles: University of California Press, 1970), pp. 43, 49, 81–83.
48. Ricoeur, "Mot," pp. 816–818.
49. See Lévi-Strauss, *Raw*, p. 3; C. Chabrol, "Problèmes de la sémiotique narrative des récits bibliques," *Langages* 6, no. 22 (June, 1971): 8–9.
50. See Lévi-Strauss, *Savage*, pp. 12, 246; *Raw*, pp. 13, 110; Edmund Leach, "The Legitimacy of Solomon: Some Structural Aspects of Old Testament History," *European Journal of Sociology* 7, no. 1 (1966): 66
51. See Barthes, "Introduction," p. 2; C. Chabrol, "Analyse du 'texte' de la Passion," *Langages* 6, no. 22 (June, 1971): 75.
52. See Roland Barthes, *Elements of Semiology*, trans. A. Lavers and C. Smith (New York: Hill and Wang, 1967), pp. 95–97; Schiwy, *Neue Aspekte,* p. 179; Piaget, *Structuralism,* pp. 3–10.
53. Barthes, *Semiology*, p. 98.
54. See Lévi-Strauss, *Raw*, p. 8; Todorov, "Poétique," pp. 154–155.
55. Barthes, *Semiology*, pp. 58–62; "Introduction," p. 3; *Essays*, pp. 205–211, 240, 243–246; Lévi-Strauss, *Raw*, p. 2.
56. Roland Barthes, *On Racine*, trans. R. Howard (New York: Hill and Wang, 1964), pp. 17–18.
57. Barthes, *Semiology*, pp. 71–74; *Essays*, pp. 205–206, 240, 243; Lévi-Strauss, *Raw*, pp. 2, 209, 306–308; Kirk, *Myth*, p. 69; Todorov, "Catégories," pp. 130–132.
58. Martin Heidegger, *Being and Time*, trans. J. Macquarrie and E. Robinson (New York and Evanston: Harper & Row, 1962), pp. 58–59.
59. Martin Heidegger, *An Introduction to Metaphysics*, trans. R. Manheim (New York: Doubleday, Anchor Book, 1961), p. 136.
60. Maurice Merleau-Ponty, *Signs*, trans. R. McCleary (Evanston: Northwestern University Press, 1964), pp. 42–43.
61. Maurice Merleau-Ponty, *The Visible and the Invisible*, trans. A. Lingis (Evanston: Northwestern University Press, 1968), p. 176.
62. Lévi-Strauss, *Anthropology*, pp. 55, 57, 198–199; Barthes, *Essays*, p. 215; Foucault, *The Order of Things*, pp. xi, 75, 362; Yves Bertherat, "La pensée folle," *Esprit* (nouvelle série), no. 360 (May, 1967): 875. Sarah N. Lawall

points out that the so-called critics of consciousness share with the structuralists their search for latent patterns behind literature. However, in her view, the critics of consciousness find in literature an end in itself, which is not the case with structuralist critics (see Sarah N. Lawall, *Critics of Consciousness* [Cambridge: Harvard University Press, 1968], pp. vii, 14–17, 172).

63. Pierre Bourdieu, "Champ intellectuel et projet créateur, *Les Temps Modernes* 22, no. 246 (November, 1966): 897–902.

64. See Schiwy, *Neue Aspekte*, p. 45.

65. Lévi-Strauss, *Anthropology*, pp. 55–56. Noam Chomsky argues that the surface structures and deep structures of sentences may be quite different. The deep structures are universal to man and account for the fact that one can produce and understand instantly sentences that are not similar to and have not been associated with sentences that he has heard. The deep structure is only represented to the mind, is implicit and not expressed. It is knowledge which is used but which one is not conscious of and cannot report on. See Noam Chomsky, *Aspects of the Theory of Syntax* (Cambridge: M.I.T. Press, 1970), pp. 8, 16, 24, 53, 57–58, 70; *Cartesian Linguistics* (New York and London: Harper & Row, 1966), pp. 33–35, 44, 59–60.

66. "Structure," p. 600.

67. See Schiwy, *Neue Aspekte*, p. 184

68. For Maurice Blanchot the literary work not only proceeds out of silence but also leads into it. The poetic word is a word of beginning, of eternal reassessment, of recommencing again and again, of essential ambiguity with its interlacing of yes and no. Therefore, the man who gives himself over to the literary word is given to a voice which does not speak; is estranged from seizable reality and truth; is consigned to indecision, to endless wandering, and to an empty, neuter existence in outer darkness. See Maurice Blanchot, *L'espace littéraire* (Paris: Editions Gallimard, 1955), pp. 307, 313, 323, 330, 333. Obviously Blanchot's view of poetic language (of the word) is at the opposite extreme from those hermeneuts (theological or otherwise) who speak of "language event."

69. Ibid., p. 5.

70. See Barthes, *Essays*, pp. 214–218. Barthes seems to contradict himself slightly when he also says (*Essays*, pp. 258–259) that the critical task is *not* to discover in the work something hidden, which had hitherto gone unnoticed, but merely to adjust the language of the critic's period (existentialism, psychoanalysis, or what have you) to the logic and language of the author's period.

71. Ibid., p. 258.

72. Todorov, "Poétique," pp. 99–103, 154; "Catégories," p. 125.

73. Lévi-Strauss, *Raw*, pp. 8, 83; *Savage*, pp. 80, 117.

74. Todorov, "Poétique," pp. 150, 154–157.

75. See Pouillon, *Présentation*, pp. 772–773; Lévi-Strauss, *Savage*, p. 250; Barthes, *Essays*, p. 215.

76. Lévi-Strauss, *Anthropology*, pp. 213–215; *Savage*, p. 81.

77. Pouillon, *Présentation*, p. 784.

78. Lévi-Strauss, *Raw*, p. 111; *Savage*, p. 136; Barthes, "Introduction," p. 27.

79. See Lévi-Strauss, *Anthropology*, pp. 209–211; Todorov, "Catégories," p. 131.

80. Lévi-Strauss, *Raw*, p. 148

81. Lévi-Strauss, *Raw*, pp. 137–138; *Anthropology*, pp. 233–236.

82. Chabrol, "Analyse," pp. 91–92.

83. Todorov, "Poétique," pp. 140–142.

84. See Erhardt Güttgemanns, "Linguistischliteraturwissenschaftliche Grund-legung einer Neutestamentlichen Theologie," *Linguistica Biblica* 13/14 (January, 1972): 5–7.

85. Lévi-Strauss, *Anthropology*, p. 221.

86. Lévi-Strauss, *Savage*, pp. 65–66, 139, 161, 263–264, 267–268; *Raw* pp. 10–13, 341.

87. Lévi-Strauss, *Raw*, pp. 92, 142.

88. See Erhardt Güttgemanns, *Offene Fragen zur Formgeschichte des Evangeliums* (München: Christian Kaiser Verlag, 1970), p. 174.

89. See Barthes, *Semiology*, pp. 38–40, 42–48; Schiwy, *Neue Aspekte*, p. 37; Chomsky, *Cartesian*, pp. 31–33.

90. See Schiwy, *Neue Aspekte*, pp. 25–26, 37–38; see also Güttgemanns, *Offene*, pp. 174–175.

91. Ricoeur, "Structure," pp. 597, 600–601, 603.

92. Barthes, *Essays*, pp. 250–251, 253–254; *Racine*, p. 163.

93. Barthes, *Racine*, p. 163.

94. Ibid.

95. Barthes, *Essays*, pp. 253–254, 258–259.

96. Ibid., pp. 259–260.

97. Robert Magliola suggests that the Barthes of *On Racine* worked with a kind of eclectic complementarity of phenomenology and structuralism, but that the Barthes of *S/Z* (1970) has become a structural purist. See Robert Magliola, "Parisian Structuralism Confronts Phenomenology: The Ongoing Debate," p. 5; unpublished paper delivered at the Modern Language As-sociation, New York, 1972.

Barthes observes that what he now does is a combination of structural and textual analysis, with text being understood as a production of significance and not as a philological object. See "La lutte avec l'ange: Analyse textuelle de Genèse 32:23–33," *Analyse Structurale et Exégèse Biblique* (Neuchâtel: Delachaux et Niestlé, 1971), p. 28. In *S/Z* (Paris: Editions du Seuil, 1970, pp. 9–12) Barthes seems to make a value judgment about what kind of text should be written today—the "writable" text—one with a galaxy of signifiers whose points of entry are unnumbered and none of which are re-jected. The text is not a structure of signifieds, and one does not choose between the possibilities of meaning: all are left at play. Thus the role of the signified seems to be reduced or eliminated, and no existential choice is made. Yet multiple meanings—perspectivism—are there, not because there is a number of possible signifieds, but because each reader must complete the signifier himself. In the case of classical texts—not writable today—Barthes concedes that we have polysemy, limited plurality, and connotation is the access to this polysemy. Here the role of the signified is acknowledged (*S/Z*, pp. 14–15). Even at times when discussing the contemporary writable text Barthes seems tacitly to grant the operation of signified or preunderstanding: the "I" who reads the text is already a plurality of other texts (ibid., p. 16). Or is the infinity of language, which transcends both the text and myself,

that which gives me access to the text and produces an infinity of readings? (Ibid., pp. 9–10, 18–19, 22–23.)
98. Barthes, *Racine*, p. 163.
99. Ibid., p. 164.
100. Ibid., pp. 165, 167, 171–172; *Essays*, p. 260. The note of "risk" in choosing an interpretation may also be found in the "critics of consciousness." See Lawall, *Critics of Consciousness*, pp. 185–186.
101. Barthes, *Racine*, pp. 8–9, 38–39, 44–49, 63–65, 72–73, 77–80, 107, 124, 126–128, 130, 136.
102. Ibid., pp. 166, 172.
103. Chabrol, "Analyse," pp. 91–92.
104. Lévi-Strauss, *Raw*, p. 341.
105. Lévi-Strauss, *Savage*, pp. 139, 217, 263–264, 267–268.
106. Raymond Picard, *New Criticism or New Fraud*, trans. F. Towne (Seattle: Washington State University Press, 1969), introduction, pages unnumbered. Barthes sometimes refers to his own criticism and that of others with similar interests as "new criticism," and that is the term which Picard uses in his attack on it. It has no connection with American "new criticism"; therefore, I have avoided the term in the hope of avoiding confusion.
107. Ibid., introduction and p. 20.
108. See E. D. Hirsch, *Validity in Interpretation* (New Haven: Yale University Press, 1967), pp. x, xi, 1, 4, 7–8, 25–26, 44–49, 66, 73–74, 77–78, 86, 89–90, 102–103, 113, 121, 139, 176, 180.
109. Ibid., pp. 18, 22, 48, 51–52, 54, 57.
110. Elizabeth Sewell, *The Orphic Voice* (New Haven: Yale University Press, 1960), p. 22.
111. See Maurice Merleau-Ponty, *Phenomenology of Perception*, trans. C. Smith (London: Routledge and Kegan Paul, 1967), pp. 9, 22, 28–30.
112. Paul Ricoeur, *De l'interprétation* (Paris: Editions du Seuil, 1965), pp. 16–17, 21–22, 25–27.
113. See Paul Ricoeur, *The Symbolism of Evil*, trans. E. Buchanan (Boston: Beacon Press, 1967), pp. 15, 51–52, 70, 86–87.
114. See Barthes, *Semiology*, p. 48.
115. See Ricoeur, *L'interprétation*, p. 40.
116. See Merleau-Ponty, *Signs*, pp. 90–92.
117. Güttgemanns, "Linguistisch," p. 2.
118. Ibid., p. 3; "Theologie," pp. 191, 193, 204, 207.
119. Güttgemanns, "Theologie," pp. 200, 220–221.
120. Ibid., p. 195.
121. Ibid., pp. 196–198.
122. Güttgemanns, "Linguistisch," pp. 5, 7, 9, 10–12; "Theologie," p. 214.
123. Güttgemanns, "Linguistisch," p. 6; "Theologie," p. 221.
124. Güttgemanns, "Theologie," pp. 213, 225–226.
125. Ibid., pp. 227–229.
126. Güttgemanns, "Linguistisch," pp. 6, 7, 14; Erhardt Güttgemanns, "Qu'est-ce que la Poétique Générative," *Linguistica Biblica* 19 (September, 1972): 4.
127. Güttgemanns, "Linguistisch," pp. 7, 13; "Theologie," pp. 228–229.
128. Chomsky, *Syntax*, pp. 16, 24, 51–53, 117; *Cartesian*, pp. 33–34.

129. This view is supported by Propp's work on the popular tale. He showed that the popular tale has some thirty functions or stable elements, and while all the functions may not appear in a given tale, the ones that do always occur in the same sequence. See Barthes, "Lutte," pp. 37–38.

130. Ernst Käsemann, "Blind Alleys in the 'Jesus of History' Controversy," *New Testament Questions of Today*, trans. W. J. Montague (Philadelphia: Fortress Press, 1969), p. 37.

131. Güttgemanns, "Linguistisch," pp. 11–12, 14, 16; "Poétique," p. 4.

132. Güttgemanns, "Linguistisch," pp. 9, 16–17.

133. Ibid., p. 17; "Theologie," pp. 219–220. According to Chomsky, while languages do not correspond in a point-for-point way and do not agree in their surface structures, there are deep-seated universals which imply that all languages are cut from the same pattern. See *Syntax*, pp. 28, 30, 118.

134. Güttgemanns, "Theologie," pp. 217–218.

135. Ibid., p. 218.

136. Ibid., pp. 202–203, 208.

137. Ibid., p. 211.

138. Edgar Haulotte, "Lisibilité des écritures," *Langages* 22 (June, 1971): 107–109.

139. Ibid., 109–112. Eduard Schweizer suggests that for the Gospel of Mark, at least, more than language-learning is necessary in order for man to understand Jesus' word as the message of the kingdom of God. Mark's point in speaking about the obscurity of the parables (chapter 4) is that one cannot grasp the reality figured in Jesus' symbolic language apart from involvement with the speaker, actualizing his understanding of existence (8:31, 34). See Eduard Schweizer, *The Good News according to Mark*, trans. D. H. Madvig (Richmond: John Knox Press, 1970), pp. 85–86, 95, 106.

140. Michael Polanyi, *Personal Knowledge* (New York: Harper & Row, Torchbooks, 1964), p. 57; *Knowing*, pp. 128, 133, 167, 170, 214.

141. Polanyi, *Personal*, p. 57; *Knowing*, pp. 128, 133–134, 140–141.

142. Polanyi, *Knowing*, pp. 140–141, 146, 214.

143. Polanyi, *Personal*, pp. 59–60; *Knowing*, p. 134.

144. Polanyi, *Personal*, 123–128; *Knowing*, pp. 134, 141, 179.

145. *Knowing*, p. 125.

146. Ibid., p. 13.

147. Barthes, "Introduction," p. 2.

148. Kirk, *Myth*, pp. 49, 50, 53, 59, 72.

149. Ibid., pp. 68, 72–73.

150. Ibid., pp. 74–75.

151. See Ricoeur, *L'interprétation*, pp. 40–44, 61–62.

152. Francis M. Cornford, *The Origin of Attic Comedy* (Cambridge: Cambridge University Press, 1934), pp. 199–200.

153. See Leach, "The Legitimacy of Solomon," p. 61.

154. Todorov, "Catégories," pp. 132, 138, 148.

155. Ricoeur, *L'interprétation*, pp. 46–47.

156. Barthes, "Introduction," p. 12.

157. Picard, *New Criticism*, pp. 33, 35–39, 41–42.

158. See Chomsky, *Syntax*, p. 70.

II

Paul and the
Comic Structure

In this chapter I shall consider three Pauline texts which expand the death-resurrection kerygma. The investigation will seek to demonstrate a *structural* relationship between Paul's theology of the death and resurrection of Jesus and the death and resurrection image in ancient Greek religion, which gave birth to comedy. This entails, let it be recalled, no effort to establish a causal-genetic relationship between Paul's theology and either Hellenistic religions or ancient Greek religion but rather a structural-generic relationship between the death-resurrection motif in Paul and that same motif which lies behind and informs classical comedy.

A. Paul and the Pre-Pauline Kerygmatic Formulas

Before turning directly to Paul we must first take a step behind him. It has been argued that the earliest form of the kerygma or pistis-formula was the bare statement "God raised him from the dead" (Rom. 10:9b). The note that the resurrection is for man's benefit Werner Kramer regards as a later addition.[1] He holds the statement that Christ died for us (cf. Rom. 5:8) also to have been an early and separate pistis-formula.[2] The statement about the resurrection was handed on by the Aramaic-speaking church to the Hellenistic Jewish church, which formulated the statement about Jesus' death as a happening for us and also combined the two in one two-part formula, thus producing such texts as 1 Cor. 15:3b–5; 1 Thess. 4:14; and the formula concealed behind 2 Cor. 5:15[3]—the kerygma which Paul inherited. Finally, Kramer holds Rom. 4:25

39

to be a probable Pauline formulation of the pre-Pauline kerygma and he also sees the basic two-part pistis-formula behind Paul's thought in Rom. 6:3–9.[4]

Now certainly Paul did inherit the two-part kerygma, but one may doubt the reliability of the pre-Pauline historical reconstruction. Even if there was a time—or a place—when only one of the two elements was proclaimed separately, this would necessarily have been an unstable and very temporary situation. I offer the following reasons for making this statement:

(1) A. J. Greimas has maintained that in the study of history we do not have the criteria to assure ourselves that structure #1 is a transformation of structure #2 and not vice versa.[5] To see the two as transformations within a larger system, whose connections are logical rather than genetic, is something else.

(2) The resurrection of Jesus could not be proclaimed without assuming his death, and it is doubtful that his death could have been regarded as "for us" apart from the resurrection.

(3) A symbol at the semantic or mythological level is always the reverse side of a larger symbolism. It seeks a signifying totality.[6] Hence death and resurrection belong together.

(4) Thinking in binary oppositions (as death/resurrection) may not be *the* structure of the human mind, but it is certainly widespread enough to be regarded as one fundamental mode of human thought.[7]

(5) Death/resurrection was a structure already in the environment of early Christianity and surely in the unconscious of Mediterranean man.

Using now the Pauline passages which I have mentioned, as well as some others to which they lead us (and without regard to their chronological relationships), let us set up a structure (to be called figure #2) which may help further the discussion. Included among these texts will be 1 Cor. 1:17–2:5, the first unit to receive a relatively full interpretation. (The symbol + indicates consecution and the symbol → indicates consequence.)

B. The Ironic Comedy of God's Foolish Wisdom

1 Cor. 1:18–2:5 is a text about the foolish wisdom of God over against the wise foolishness of the world. Into this paradox Paul

takes his concept of the word of God—its content, its style and mode of being preached, and the church which it calls into existence. Thus it is as much a text about the word or kerygma as about God.

One may plausibly contend that the unit here is 1:18–3:23 because 3:4–17 refers again to the parties mentioned in 1:10–17, and 3:18–23 returns to the beginning point of 1:18—God's paradoxical wisdom.[8] Nevertheless, it can be argued convincingly that 1:18–2:5 is a discrete subunit because at 2:6 Paul departs from the theme of the paradoxical wisdom or foolishness.

Prior to 1:18 Paul has been rehearsing some of the past history of his relationship with the Corinthian church, and he has been speaking in the first person. This brings him (at 1:17) to a statement about his sense of the main purpose of his calling—to preach—and also anticipates the content of that preaching. Therefore, 1:17 is a transition verse between his first person narrative about his relationship with the church and a third person "semi-narrative" about what might be called "the destiny of the word" (1:18–31), which, it will be argued, reflects the comic form and point of view. Paul's return to first person ("I") narration in 2:1–5 will be discussed below. Note that in 1:23 and 1:30 Paul uses the first person *plural*. But the "we" of 1:23 is probably a reflection of the confessional style;[9] moreover, the first person plural from the standpoint of linguistics is not simply an increase in the number of "I" 's but rather entails a different logic.[10]

At this stage I should clarify that I am using the terms comedy and comic in the sense of a form or structure which embodies certain thematic meanings and not in the sense of what is funny or laughable.[11] Recall that while myth is dominant in tragedy it is logos—theme or idea—which is most prominent in comedy.[12] Thus a comic view is more amenable than tragedy to a representation which is only semi-narrative. Even so, in 1 Cor. 1:18ff the structure (modified) of death-resurrection, and its consequences, is there.

My procedure now will be to give a brief interpretation of 1 Cor. 1:18–2:5 along structuralist lines and then to show how it participates in the comic genre. In this passage it is God who acts (1:19, 27–30) but he acts *through* the kerygma (1:21); therefore, the word stands out in the text as God's active power (1:18), and that is the keynote. The word acts to save and to destroy, to make a division between men but, as we shall see, that is to state the matter too simply.

According to Conzelmann, Paul's intention here is to present the cross as the exhaustive content of his word (1:17, 23; 2:2). Paul did not need to convince the Corinthians of the resurrection. He rather wanted to represent the form in which we have the resurrected one—as the crucified.[13] Thus Conzelmann explains the failure of the resurrection to be mentioned here by reference to the historical situation, which may well be part of the truth, but may not the text itself bear on the question as well as its relationship to its total genre-structure?

FIGURE #2

syntagm→	1	2	3	4	5	6	7
Rom. 10:9b				Christ's resurrection+			salvation for man
Rom. 5:8			Christ's death +				for man
1 Thess. 4:14			Christ's death	Christ's resurrection			man's future resurrection
2 Cor. 5:15			Christ's death +	Christ's resurrection			for man
1 Cor. 15:3b–5			Christ's death +	Christ's resurrection	according to Scriptures		for man's sins
Rom. 4:25			Christ's death +	Christ's resurrection			for man's justification
Rom. 5:12–18	Adamic (racial) + sin & death	Christ's obedient→ struggle					justification and life
Phil. 2:8–11		Christ's humble + obedience	Christ's death +	Christ's exaltation→			
Rom. 6:3–10		Christ's death = to sin	Christ's death +	Christ's resurrection	+	death of sinful self	life and future resurrection
Cor. 1:17–2:5	boastful wisdom of→ world		Christ's death +	power of word	according to Scriptures	shattering of wise + boastful man	life and true wisdom for man

↑ paradigm

Figure #2 demonstrates the tendency of both the pre-Pauline church and Paul to make use of a binary formula, death/ressur·rection. As suggested before, there is a strong general tendency in man to think in binary oppositions. Since, in the resurrection paradigm, the power of the word has replaced the resurrection in

1 Cor. 1:18ff., we are led to the conclusion that cross/resurrection has been transformed into the formula cross/word; therefore, the resurrection is seen *as* the power of the word. Paul is still using a binary formula, and the cross is not the exhaustive content of his kerygma. The power of the kerygma itself is a part of the content. The word or kerygma is not just words with which he can proclaim or reflect on the cross or the cross/resurrection; it is also itself something whose power he can proclaim and on which he can reflect with other words, with (theological) metalanguage.

In 1:26–29 Paul reminds the Corinthian church that it is as lowly and foolish as the crucified Christ and that, as such, God has chosen it to shame the strong boasters (the world) and to bring to nothing things that are. But the fact that he states that no one is to boast in the presence of God and reminds the church (*humeis*) and himself (*hēmin*) that God is the source of their (our) life, wisdom, and redemption means that he is not simply designating the Corinthian church as the lowly and weak whom God has chosen in order to shame and to bring to naught the strong. It means that Paul is also reminding the church that they who were once the strong and boastful have been brought to nothing in order that they might be saved: the gift of life in 1:30 follows the destruction of the self-sufficient attitude described in 1:27–29. This view is confirmed by the fact that Paul says that God has consigned *all* to disobedience in order that he might have mercy on all (Rom. 11:32) and by the related idea—presented from the standpoint of the individual man (see figure #2)—that the old self is crucified in order to open up the way to life (Rom. 6:6–8). In 1 Cor. 1:26–30 the crushing and saving of man are simply juxtaposed, but that life is the ultimate *intention* of death is suggested by the paradigm (6) in figure #2.

In 1 Cor. 2:1–5 Paul asserts that the humble and unadorned style and manner of his proclamation is appropriate to the offensive and foolish content of the word of the cross. But however much Paul may have thought so, the word which he speaks about in 2:1–5 is not exactly the same as the one in 1:18ff. In 1:18ff. he speaks of the word in a third person narration, and third person narration refers to a constant, invariant, objective notion. But in 2:1–5 he returns to first person narration whose only referent is the present discourse which "I" am now articulating.[14] The word of 1:18ff. is the power of God determining the saved and the perishing. In 2:1–5 it is that by which Paul's "I" is defined.

In the passage 1 Cor. 1:18–2:5 we do not see in the foreground man moving through dissolution to newness, but rather the controlling factor throughout is the word. Not only is man's experience contained in the destiny of the word, but the word functions as the power of God and the resurrected Christ. God and Christ are experienced through the word.

FIGURE #3

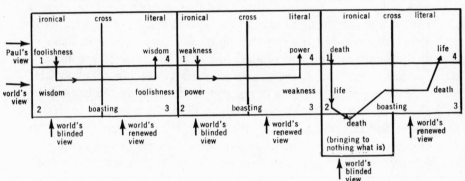

The syntagm of 1 Cor. 1:18–2:5 in figure #2 may be formalized differently (see figure #3) as four binary oppositions: foolishness/wisdom; weakness/power; death/life; cross/boasting. In each four-block square, blocks #1 and #4 reveal Paul's double or paradoxical attitude toward the cross, and blocks #2 and #3 reveal the world's changing attitude toward boasting. The arrows inside the blocks represent God's (the word's) acting toward the world, apparently in opposition but actually in redemption; for the world, by having its self-understanding and status in existence reversed, is removed from death to life. Thus the world changes its understanding not only of boasting but also of the cross (blocks #2–#1–#3–#4), and is brought around to the viewpoint of the gospel (Paul). Block #3 in each case represents the gospel's single view of boasting, although this block is found in the world's axis.

God's foolishness confronts the world's wisdom showing the latter to be foolishness, thus revealing God's foolishness as wisdom. The same is true of the weakness/power opposition. In the death/life square a paradigm must be formed for death on the world's axis because death has two meanings in the text. It is not only the cross of Christ but also the existential death of man, the death of the old self. God's death (the cross) confronts the world's life (self-sufficient boasting) bringing this false life to nothing (death) and therefore disclosing that false life as real death and the cross, which shatters it, as the way of life.

In 1914 Francis Cornford wrote a monumental book on Aristophanes and the origins of Attic comedy. One of his concerns was to demonstrate certain historical connections, but he handled his materials so deftly that much of his work is usable for structural analysis, and Cornford is today sometimes spoken of as a structuralist before structuralism.[15] The essence of his historical position is that literary comedy (in Aristophanes) emerged from folk drama which in turn was derived from an ancient fertility ritual which included a sacred marriage to enhance the fertility of the land and some kind of motif involving the removal of an old king-god and the appearance of a new one or the death of the old king and his resurrection and renewal.[16] This view of the origins of comedy is still basically maintained by a number of more recent writers.[17]

The fundamental structure of Aristophanic comedy as established by Cornford is schematically set forth as follows:[18]

(1) The first major episode is the agon in which the agonist-hero engages in a struggle or contest with an antagonist and wins a victory.

(2) Then he enjoys the fruits of his victory while offering a *sacrifice* and celebrating a *feast*.

(3) Finally the hero leads a victory procession—*komos*—and enters into some kind of marriage and experiences a resurrection of some sort.

The agonist-hero is often an *eiron* (ironical man) who feigns stupidity and makes himself out to be less than he is. But in the end his shrewd humility proves to be wisdom.[19] Contrasted with him is *alazon* or imposter—a boastful, foolish pretender—who usually appears after the agon, claiming an undeserved share in the fruits of victory. His fate is to be rebuffed and chased away. He is a kind of double of the chief antagonist who may himself be an alazon.[20]

As Cornford points out, old Attic comedy does not turn on romantic love, and nothing in the plot accounts for the appearance of the woman at the end in readiness for the marriage. Thus her advent is a survival from the ancient fertility ritual.[21] In structuralist terms, an element that cannot be accounted for at the syntagmatic level is explained by recourse to the paradigm.

What may we now say briefly and synthetically about the comic spirit through the years? If comedy began without romantic love, it has hardly ever since that time been without it.[22] It gives us a healthy release from the serious professions and authority to which we usually feel responsible but occasionally resent.[23] Comedy gives us the staying power to come back and reminds us that no matter how many times we are knocked down we can pick ourselves up again.[24] To the (possibly) tragic episodes of birth, struggle, and death comedy adds resurrection and the sense of the infinite, working in man with no outward signs; therefore, comedy is the only complete and fulfilled mode of action.[25] It offers us a sense of the regain of what we feared we had lost.[26] The comic spirit is the "pure sense of life" and celebration and maintaining our balance, which grows out of the elemental human rhythm of upset and recovery.[27]

Comedy and tragedy, as we know, work with the same materials and comedy achieves its effect by reversing or inverting the roles of tragedy. More specifically it is the Oedipal situation reversed. The guilt which in the tragedy rests on the son is diverted to the father. The son plays the role of the victorious father with his sexual freedom and achievement while the father becomes a frustrated onlooker or is reduced to a son.[28]

Figure #4 reproduces a part of figure #2 plus an additional Pauline text and four syntagms representing Aristophanic plays. Despite the highly illuminating character of Cornford's work his statement about the basic structure of Aristophanes' comedy tends to be a kind of common denominator. It will be more helpful, I think, to build four of the actual plays into the genre-structure-system which we are constructing. Note that in Aristophanes' comedies the hero suffers a kind of symbolic death during the agon and anticipates the "resurrection" which is more fully realized at the end. In Paul, on the other hand, the actual death of Christ occurs just after the agon and is stressed much more than is death in the Aris-

FIGURE #4

syntagm→ 1	2	3	4	5	6	7	8
Rom. 5:12–18 — Adamic (racial) sin and death	Christ's obedient struggle						justification and life
Phil. 2:8–11	Christ's humble + obedience	Christ's death	Christ's exaltation				
1 Cor. 11:23–26		Christ's death	resurrection implied		bread **and** cup		
1 Cor. 1:17–2:5 — boastful wisdom of world		Christ's death	power of word	according to Scripture		agon: eiron-god shatters alazon-world	gaining of life and true wisdom for man
Birds	agon	sacrifice				second agon	komos: hero hailed as young god; marriage feast
Clouds	agon				feast	agon— defeat of alazon	komos: hero wins victory over his own foolishness as well as over alazon
Plutus	agon				feast	defeat of alazon	komos: new Zeus and marriage
Frogs	agon				feast	agon: between two alazons	komos: victor returned from Hades to life.

paradigm

tophanic plays. The resurrection in the last paradigm in Paul is not the resurrection of Christ, which has already occurred, but the "resurrection" of others with him, which corresponds to the participation of the worshipers in the original ritual from which the drama came and to the possible effect of the play on the audience.

The apparent tendency of 1 Cor. 1:18–29, except for a few hints to the contrary, is to represent the classical, tragic Oedipal situation. The powerful, wise father (God) shames and brings to naught the guilty, weak son (world). But in 1:30 the introduction of the strong note of life and redemption clearly reverses the tragic tendency. This then leads us to reconsider the whole passage in the light of what we have learned about the comic structure and spirit.

Let us refer again to two comic motifs: (1) The free son is victorious over the guilty father; (2) the self-depreciating and apparently foolish eiron-hero is finally victorious over the boastful alazon.

In 1 Cor. 1:18–31 both of these motifs are at work so that we do not have merely the inversion of the tragic situation into the theme of the victorious son and defeated father. Rather the two motifs are merged and both roles are reconstituted so that neither of the "characters" is in the end just what he is in, say, Aristophanic comedy. Mediating between the victorious hero and the defeated alazon is the paradox of life through death. God identifies himself with the lowly and despised—the crucified Christ and the church— and thus becomes an eiron, and the world (son) is a boastful alazon. The alazon is shown that his wisdom is really a foolish illusion (that he can dispose of his own existence); therefore, the crushing of the guilty son turns out to be the crushing of his existence in illusion and self-deception, and he is really thereby freed for life and wisdom. The irony of God is that he enters into (he saves through the foolish kerygma) the suffering and humiliation (the cross) caused by man's illusion (that he runs the world) and thereby shatters that illusion. But God's victory, which is the defeat of the alazon-world, ironically is the victory of man as freedom for new life. Thus the eiron-hero-God does not simply win a victory for himself over the alazon and chase the latter away. While man prior to being brought to naught by the eiron-God was a combination of the guilty son of tragedy and the alazon of comedy, after his "defeat" he is the free son of comedy, but a son who is reconciled to rather than victorious over his father. It may be true, as Susanne Langer[29] says, that the hero of comedy does not change. But it is also certainly true that for "Pauline comedy" the ironical action of the hero effects a radical change in the alazon.

Finally before leaving this passage I should like to raise two questions which can be given only provisional answers. The first is: On what grounds does Paul affirm that *God* is identified with the cross, that God *chose* the weak and low and despised? One could as easily—or more easily—conclude from the event of the crucifixion that God is cruel or that there is no God. Perhaps the clue to Paul's opposite conclusion is his experience of and reflection on the word, through which he comes to Christ and God. The word is experienced as the power to give life, and power is experienced as he who is God. Or, because the word is experienced as the word of life, it is interpreted as the word of God. If God is experienced in the word of the cross which makes power present, then God must have been present in the cross.

But why is this particular word experienced as the effective life-giving word? Perhaps because it is a particularly gripping representation of the comic view. Death/resurrection is the image which stands at the heart of the comic form. As an image it arises from the heart and soul of man, from those levels beneath the conscious, and when it strikes the hearer or reader it breaks through his consciousness and reaches the depths of the unconscious where it sets up reverberations and resonances.[30] May we not say that these reverberations put man at the unconscious level in touch—at least potentially—with all that belongs to the comic structure, and reflection, as well as living itself, will hopefully bring it to consciousness, as a dialectic is set up between the unconscious and the conscious. These reverberations move us into a participation in that pure sense of life which runs the gamut from romantic love, to escapism, to a power that can turn crucifixion into renewal. Not only is a Pauline text to be interpreted in the light of other Pauline texts and in connection with the cultural-religious environment, but every element in a Pauline syntagm is to be read from the vantage point of its paradigm. By showing that the New Testament kerygma belongs to the structure of comedy we can see why that which is most elemental in the Christian proclamation sets up reverberations in that rhythm of life which is most elemental in man as such.

C. The Comedy of Justification and the Resurrection Situation

The next text to be considered at some length is Rom. 9:30–10:21, which is a part of the larger section 9:1–11:36. In 9:1–29 Paul emphasizes God's action specifically as determining the identity of the saved Israel, and toward the end he has mentioned the inclusion of the gentiles. Beginning with 9:30, however, and running through 10:21 the stress shifts to the contrasting attitudes of the Jews and gentiles toward the proclaimed word. At 11:1 Paul turns to the different but related question of whether Israel is to be permanently rejected. These remarks plus the structural analysis to follow show, then, that 9:30–10:21 is a self-contained text.

In contrast to 1 Cor. 1:18–2:5 the resurrection is mentioned in Rom. 9:30ff., but in the latter text it is God who sends the preachers of the word and the word which acts as the instrument effecting the salvation event—faith (10:8, 17). Thus, here, as in 1 Corinthians 1, the word really functions as the resurrected Christ. Moreover, in both cases the word divides men into two groups, the saved (believers) and the perishing. However, in 1 Cor. 1:18ff. the narrative form is comic, ending on the note of life and justification, while in Rom. 9:30ff. the narrative form is tragic, the last word being Israel's disobedience. We may remind ourselves that comedy and tragedy deal with the same situation in different ways and both arise from the same nuclear opposition: death/resurrection. The two genres diverge depending on whether they place the emphasis on the element of death (tragedy) or the element of marriage and resurrection (comedy).[31]

According to Claude Bremond there are two fundamental narrative processes—the process of amelioration (what I have called comic) and the process of degradation or damaging (what I have called tragic). He has further pointed out that the basic narrative sequence, which can be expanded and developed in various ways, is one composed of three functions. The first function initiates a process which has a goal; and with regard to functions two and three the author has a choice between two alternative ways of proceeding.[32] In order to see Rom. 9:30–10:21 represented under this model, note figure #5, observing that at function three Paul chooses *both* alternatives.

FIGURE #5

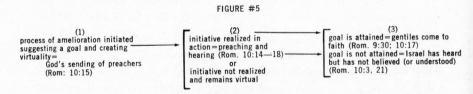

Rom. 9:30–10:21 may also be represented as a syntagm in the genre-structure we are developing (see figure #6), suggesting that

FIGURE #6

syntagm ——→

	1	2	3	4	5	6	7	8
Aristophanes		agon	sacrifice	power of word		feast	agon	komos: marriage and resurrection
1 Cor. 1:17–2:5	boastful wisdom of world		Christ's death	resurrection understood as operation of word	according to Scripture		agon: eiron-God shatters alazon-world	gaining of life; and true wisdom for man
Rom. 9:30–10:21	Israel's pursuit of righteous-ness of law		Christ's death	resurrection understood as operation of word			Israel's failure to respond	gentiles brought to faith
Rom. 4			death: barren hopelessness of sterility / Christ's death	promise of God / Christ's resurrection				faith of Abraham—justification of man
Deuteronomy	Israel's rebellion (1:26–28; 9:6–17; 32:15–18)	Moses' struggle with Israel and with God for Israel (1:12; 3:25–27; 9:17–19; 10:10)	sacrifices: (12:11–12; 27:7); Moses' death "for Israel" (3:25–27; 32:50–51; 34:5)	Moses' life-giving word is to confront Israel after his death (8:3; 31:28–32:2)		feasts: (16:1–17; 14:22–27)	Israel is destroyed	Israel is given life
Hosea	harlotry and rebellion of Israel (1:2; 2:5–6; 11:2)	Hosea reenacts Israel's struggle with God	Hosea experiences abandonment (2:2)	the whole book is word (1:1; 4:1; 5:1)			God destroys (11:5–7; 6:1)	God restores (11:8–9; 6:1–2)

paradigm

while its narrative form is tragic, it may still be assimilated to the logic of comedy. In this case Israel's pursuit of the righteousness of the law is a correlative of the Corinthians' self-sufficient wisdom. Israel's failure to believe is a hardening of her legal self-sufficiency (see Rom. 9:18; 11:7–10). The word can harden a man as well as shatter his boastful security; therefore, operation 7 in 1 Cor.

1:18–2:5 has been transformed into its opposite in operation 7 in Rom. 9:30–10:21.

If Romans 10 (see figure #5) is taken apart from Romans 11 and the theme of Israel's failure to believe is backed up by such passages as 1 Thess. 5:2–3; 1 Cor. 6:9–10; Gal. 5:21, then Paul must have seen Israel's (man's) lostness as a permanent possibility. If, however, Romans 10 is seen in the light of Romans 11, then Israel's lostness is temporary.

Also, if (in figure #6) Israel's hardened unbelief (operation 7) is viewed only in the light of its own syntagm, Israel (some men) remains in unbelief while other men (gentiles) are turned to faith. But, if Israel's unbelief (operation 7) is regarded as a continuation (intensified) of the legal self-security of operation 1, and the whole syntagm of Rom. 9:30ff. is considered against the background of the total structure, then operation 7 from 1 Cor. 1:18ff. can be expected to "drop down" into the syntagm of Rom. 9:30ff. and finally to shatter Israel in her hardened legal self-security for the sake of her salvation. One is tempted to conclude that Paul at times consciously believed that some men would be eternally lost, but that belief is at variance with the comic structure which seems really to have governed his thought and which has sufficient breadth finally to overcome the notion of eternal lostness.

The highly interesting passage, Rom. 10:6–10, elaborates the operation—according to the Scriptures—which came to Paul from the kerygma of the church before him. Käsemann's analysis of Paul's hermeneutic uses this passage as a test case. Käsemann organizes his discussion around the contrast which Paul makes between letter and spirit. According to Käsemann, Paul saw the law in its origin and intention as the sacred will of God calling men to obedience and offering a promise. The Jewish tradition has perverted the law into letter—a demand for good works—and this tradition or usage is a veil which blinds the reader of the Old Testament and makes him hear it as a demand for good works (see Rom. 7:6; 2 Cor. 3:6).[33]

For Käsemann the spirit also has a hermeneutical function. It has a bearing on Scripture as something given beforehand, but like letter it is also something which can be derived from Scripture.[34] Käsemann then proceeds to state that Paul (in Rom. 10:6–10) saw different meanings in Lev. 18:5 and Deut. 30:11–14. Paul, unlike Philo, did not spiritualize Scripture but rather drew a dividing line setting Scripture against Scripture. Some parts of the Old Testament have become meaningless for Paul while he took up others over and over again; the criterion for the real and true word was justification by faith. Paul's question was: where in the Old Testament can the word of justification be heard?[35]

In response to Käsemann we must declare that the criterion of justification by faith led Paul, to a degree, to misinterpret Deut. 30:11–14. Käsemann has really not probed the question *why* Paul might have found justification by faith in Deut. 30:11–14 but not in Lev. 18:5. Nor does he deal with the initiative which the Old Testament may have exercised on Paul, along with affording him a series of texts in which he could find his own theme of justification. Beyond these points there are a number of obscurities in Käsemann's position.

What exactly is the hermeneutical role of the spirit? How is it that the spirit has a bearing on Scripture but also can be derived from it?

How is the hermeneutical role of the spirit in Paul related to the meaning of the spirit in primitive Christianity—the divine energy of miracle and ecstasy?[36]

What is the relationship of the hermeneutical role of the spirit to the hermeneutical role of justification by faith?

What do letter and spirit have in common which makes it possible to contrast them?

I will begin by seeking a solution to the last question and then proceed to work through the others. The juxtaposition of letter and spirit represents a classical example of the *elementary structure of signification*. The latter is composed of two elements in relationship which have something in common (conjunction) but which are also opposed to each other in some way (disjunction). In order to analyze the nature of this elementary structure of signification we must clarify three factors.[37]

The elements in the structure may be "terms," that is, lexemes (words) in an empirical natural language which are grasped by perception.

The terms have properties or qualities or elements of signification (units of the signified) which are called "sems." In the light of this we may further define a term or lexeme as a collection of sems, and we may observe that the structure may be regarded as a relation of sems as well as of terms.

The "semantic axis" is that which arranges or holds together the two opposing terms, or sems. It is the common denominator which makes the two terms comparable, the dimension in which the opposition is manifested. The axis is the semantic content of the relation between the two (or more) terms or sems, which joins and subsumes the elements which may be analytically disengaged from it in their likenesses and differences. This is not to say that the axis is given. It is rather the terms which are given, and the articulation of the axis and the sems is a metalinguistic activity, a reflective creation of a discourse upon a discourse (the terms).

If we begin with the binary opposing terms boy/girl, the axis is sex and the sems are masculinity and femininity. If the terms are long/short or wide/narrow, the axis is relative quantity and the sems are great quantity (whose terms are long and wide) and small quantity (whose terms are short and narrow). Our given terms are letter and spirit and our metalinguistic task is to discover and articulate the axis, or axes, from which the sems may be disengaged.

The text of 2 Cor. 3:6 may suggest that the axis for letter/spirit is covenant. Thus the sems for our two terms would be two characterizations of life in the covenant. In the covenant of the letter one is an enslaved minor heir destined for death, while in the covenant of the spirit one is a free, inheriting son destined for life (2 Cor. 3:6; Gal. 3:15, 17, 25–26, 28; 4:1, 7, 8, 24, 26, 31; 5:1).

It may also be true that the two terms are arranged along the axis law. When the law is approached from the point of pertinence or preunderstanding, justification by works, then the law is seen as letter, as demand for good works which will justify (Rom. 7:6–7; 2:6, 25; Gal. 3:2, 10–12). But when the law is approached from the preunderstanding justification by faith, then the law is spirit (Rom. 8:2). It is the law of Christ (Gal. 6:2).[38] The law in its original intention—ontologically—is life-giving (Rom. 7:10) as is spirit (2 Cor. 3:6). Pointing man to his finitude (Rom. 7:7) may point him to God, the source of righteousness and life (Rom. 9:31–32).[39] Thus the sems for letter and spirit on the axis law are preunderstanding as the demand for meritorious works and preunderstanding as a pointer to God as life-giver. In the process of coming to this conclusion we have also discovered that pre-understanding as content is the axis for justification by faith/justification by works, although these may also be *new* under-standing as well.

Let us consider one more axis for letter/spirit. For Paul the letter is a veil which holds man captive (2 Cor. 3:6, 14; Rom. 7:6) and kills him (2 Cor. 3:6). That is, it locks him into his old self-understanding. The spirit=the Lord (2 Cor. 3:17), and the resurrected Lord=the word (1 Cor. 1:18, 21; Rom. 10:8, 17); therefore, the spirit equals the word. The spirit is the revealer which removes the veil (2 Cor. 3:3, 16–17) and gives freedom and life (2 Cor. 3:6, 17). The spirit is the word in its power to spring the old self-understanding and enable one to see oneself anew in relation to Christ and the Old Testament. The spirit is the word which can write itself on the heart of man and thus "re-write" man as a new being (2 Cor. 3:1–3). The spirit as the power of the word thus reveals its relationship to the older idea of the spirit as the power of miracle and ecstasy (Gal. 3:5; 1 Cor. 12:1, 9–10).

The third axis for letter/spirit, then, is preunderstanding as power, and the sems are power to lock in and to kill and power to rewrite into newness. Let us recall that the axis for the two kinds of justification is preunderstanding as content. We may relate the hermeneutical function of spirit/letter and justification by faith/justification by works in the following way. Spirit is the power of the word of justification by faith to open up the Scripture and give life, while the letter is the power of the motif of justification by works to veil the truth and kill.

We see in conclusion that the term letter has gathered the sems: enslaved minor heir destined for death, preunderstanding as justification by works, power to lock in and kill. On the other hand, the term spirit has collected the sems: free inheriting son destined for life, preunderstanding as justification by faith, power to rewrite in newness.

Since spirit and letter are terms of the axes law and covenant and also of the axis preunderstanding we may see in these terms the dialectic between the text (Old Testament) and the preunderstanding.

Spirit is also the power of preunderstanding to understand the gospel of the cross as well as to understand the Old Testament. The spirit (1 Cor. 2:10–13) leads to the maturity and wisdom (1 Cor. 2:6), to recognize the foolishness of the cross as genuine (God's) wisdom (1 Cor. 1:18, 21, 24, 25), to be led past a false wisdom which is really folly into true wisdom (1 Cor. 3:18–20).

If justification by faith is preunderstanding as content in reference to the Old Testament, then in reference to the gospel of the cross, whose content is justification by faith (the crushing of man in order to save him), the fact that the spirit makes it possible to see this as wisdom and not as folly means that the gospel of justification has power to authenticate itself.

It can authenticate itself, however, because of a certain point of contact in man. Romans 1–2 suggests that man has a point of contact for God's revelation, but it has been distorted. Can that point of contact not be a deep structure of the mind—the comic genre—whose distortion is being rectified by the gospel and turned into particular channels inherent in the gospel? At the same time that fundamental structure of the mind, the comic genre, channels the expression of the gospel. The basic sense of human life expressed by the comic genre—the rhythm of upset and recovery—however distorted, enables the gospel to strike a responsive note, to reverberate through the human psyche.

Paul proclaims the gospel because the kerygma confronted him in his history as language event; then the comic genre influenced the way in which he expresses his elaboration of the kerygma. The Christian kerygma has to do with the most radical and fundamental upset and recovery (death and resurrection, life through death), and by it all other expressions of this rhythm are judged. At the same time other expressions of the comic sense of life give significance to the death-resurrection kerygma and provide it with a point of contact.

To recapitulate: Paul preaches his kerygma because he has been encountered by the proclamation of the death and resurrection of

Jesus. But the belongingness of important Pauline texts to the comic genre shows that that structure shaped his articulation of the kerygma and his theology. The comic genre-structure is in its essence the awareness (tacit or explicit) of the rhythm of upset and recovery. This interpretation of what was going on in Paul's theologizing is confirmed by the fact that Paul retranslates the message of the cross and resurrection—or Christian existence as living the death and resurrection of Jesus—back into the fundamental human experience of upset and recovery (2 Cor. 4:7–11; 6:3–10). The historical particularity of the resurrected Christ as word rearranges Paul's self-understanding and activates by reverberation the working of the comic genre (because death and resurrection are central also to that genre) which in turn generates Paul's performance texts (actualized statements), although one would not want to rule out the contribution of Paul's historical situation to the content of those texts.

A full discussion of Rom. 10:6–10 might begin by taking issue with the opinion of Jack Suggs that the phrase "the righteousness based on faith" is only a "stylistic flourish" employed to help Paul's interpretation.[40] I contend rather that Paul speaks in this fashion because he sees righteousness by faith to be an Old Testament structure of meaning as well as a Christian one. He must have since he posits it of Abraham in Romans 4. Since Paul sees this structure in the Old Testament, when he states here that "the righteousness of faith says," he means that this motif speaking in the Old Testament says. Thus he is saying something here about his understanding of the Old Testament and of the redemptive possibilities in history before Christ, and therefore the statement is not just a rhetorical flourish. In view of the trend of my argument it seems appropriate to present at this point a discussion of Romans 4 before proceeding with Rom. 10:6–10.

In Romans 4 Paul is giving proof from Scripture for the theme of the righteousness of faith, which he has expounded in Rom. 3:21–31. There would be no point to this argument if Abraham's faith did not anticipate Christian faith and was not ultimately identical with it.[41] We may say, then, that Paul posits a "resurrection situation" in Abraham's history and a corresponding faith arising out of it.[42] Paul has reinterpreted the past (Abraham) in the light of the present (the Christian experience of the death and resurrection of Jesus); by the same token what he discerns in the Abraham story may well have contributed to his understanding of the resurrection of Jesus. This dialectical relationship is seen in the fact that his discussion of Abraham moves immediately to a kerygmatic statement about Jesus' death and resurrection for man's justification, and figure #6 shows the two situations to be structurally parallel.

In Romans 4 God's speaking godless Abraham into righteousness, his promising heirs to old and sterile parents, his giving life to the dead, and his calling into existence things which are not (4:5, 13, 17, 19) are all correlatives of each other.[43] The resurrection situation is the promise of life in the midst of death, and if the word brings this life to existence then the structure of the word must qualify the structure of the life.

The subjective quality of faith is perhaps more in evidence and more succinctly defined in Romans 4 than in Romans 10 or 1 Corinthians 1. It is trusting in God where the natural inclination of man is to trust himself (Rom. 4:5; Phil. 3:4–11). It is holding in hope to the promise of God when the situation in the world denies the possibility of its fulfillment. Even this faith is not man's achievement. It is the consequence of that crucifixion of the self-justifying self, that bringing of that which is to nothing,[44] which is only hinted at in Romans 4 in the suggestion that Abraham, too, was ungodly (4:5), but which is presupposed because of its place in Paul's total genre-structure (figure #6, paradigm 7). Faith then is the subjective situation of the alazon after he has been deflated —that is, saved—by the eiron-God. With the qualification already indicated, faith and justification represent the subjective and objective aspects of the situation of the saved man (figure #6, operation 8 of Romans 4).

The broader import of Romans 4 seems to be that for Paul the death-resurrection-faith situation is a possibility—ontologically and ontically—at any point along the line of the history of salvation. Yet Paul also speaks of a time before faith came and of faith's coming with the coming of Christ (Gal. 3:23–25). Käsemann reconciles these two positions very nicely by pointing out that salvation history is the history of God's word which is able to evoke faith, and as such it is not marked by visible and earthly continuity but by interruptions and paradox.[45] Thus the "before faith came" refers not to the fact that there had been no occasions of faith before Christ came but that they had come intermittently and separated by gaps. There were times of faith before Christ, but there were also always times before faith came.

If the Christian word, which participates in the comic genre-structure, is able to arouse faith, can the same power be denied in principle to any other substructure which represents that genre?

And so we return to Rom. 10:6–10. Jack Suggs works with the view that Paul in 1 Corinthians drew upon a Jewish wisdom tradition in order to identify Christ and wisdom, which Judaism identified with the law.[46] This enabled Paul to articulate a more positive relationship between law and gospel than he had before. Paul's use of Deuteronomy parallels the treatment of wisdom in Bar. 3:29–30. Heaven and the abyss were proverbial terms for the inaccessibility of wisdom, and late Judaism used Deut. 30:11–14 to show that God had brought it near in the Torah.[47]

The familiar heaven-abyss manner of describing wisdom in her hiddenness apparently influenced Paul's citation of the Deuteronomy passage, according to Suggs. By thus identifying Christ with the wisdom-Torah Paul was able to resolve the tension between gospel and law. To obey Christ in faith is to obey the law in truth.[48] Apparently Suggs means that the reference to the death and resurrection of Jesus made a point of contact with the abyss-heaven theme in the wisdom speculations which made use of Deut. 30:11–14.

By rejoinder I would suggest that the Christ-wisdom-law equation may have been a part of Paul's conscious thought. But one may argue that it was the importance of the word in Paul's theology which was the most direct contact with the Deuteronomy text where the term *word* is also used. The basic content of Paul's word—death and resurrection—led him to grasp, perhaps rather unconsciously, certain parallels between the structure of his own thought and that of Deuteronomy.

One may question whether Paul's identification of Christ with the law-wisdom really relieved the tension between law and gospel. Has it not rather pushed the tension back into the law itself, drawing that line which Käsemann speaks of and setting Scripture against Scripture? The law contains moments of gospel, points at which the word of justification by faith is heard, and this is what the law "in truth" is, as distinguished from the law as letter. Given the binary nature of Paul's thought—works/faith, letter/spirit, etc.—when he says that the word of justification, the word of death and resurrection, is internal (Rom. 10:8), he implies that the law (as letter) is external (2 Cor. 3:1–6).

The overall meaning of Rom. 10:5–10 is, then, something like this: The righteousness of faith, speaking in the Old Testament, says: Do not seek the crucified-risen Christ in a cosmically distant point, but seek him in the near word which, entering your heart, brings you to saving faith. Since this word is the meaning of saving history —or is saving history—encountering man potentially at any point in that history (as in the Abraham story or in Deuteronomy), the meaning of the text is: Let yourself see the death and resurrection at any of the nodal points of that history and let yourself be borne into that history by what it says to you.

We are now ready at last to confront the question: Since Lev. 18:5 refers to the law, and since the term *word* in Deut. 30:11–14 also refers to the law, why *did* Paul see the Leviticus passage to represent justification by works and the Deuteronomy text to represent the righteousness of faith?

Both Leviticus and Deuteronomy present a series of oppositions each of which reflects in some way the opposition life/death (for a selected presentation of these oppositions see figures #7 and #8). In each of the books there is also an opposition with regard to the means of salvation or of effecting atonement, that is, how mediation between death and life takes place.[49]

FIGURE #7—Leviticus

clean	near	obedience	keep land	life	
unclean	far	disobedience	lose land	death	blood

FIGURE #8—Deuteronomy

hear	obey	know	remember	clean	possess land	live	
not listen	disobey	be deceived	forget	unclean	perish from land	die	word

In Leviticus Israel acquires life and maintains herself in the land by obedience to the law, both cultic and moral (18:5; 20:22; 23:11; 26:3–39). On the other hand, atonement is provided by the sacrificial blood of the cult which God has given (Lev. 17:11). Von Rad has pointed out that the Priestly writer was very concerned about the external correctness of offering sacrifices but made almost no effort to explain their meaning beyond the slight but not very far-reaching hint in Lev. 17:11.[50] Leviticus points out that the life is in the blood and blood should, therefore, not be eaten (17:14). Blood, as that which mediates between life and death, is the life of the animal released by its death, and, offered on the altar, it leads from threatened death to the life of the people and possession of the land. In line with this theme of cultic grace in Leviticus is the occasional suggestion that obedience is a response to God or a reflection of his holiness (22:31–33; 25:55; 19:2), rather than a condition for or means of acquiring life. In summary the two opposing ways of moving from death to life are the obedience of Israel and the cultic act of God.

Deuteronomy also speaks of the life as residing in the blood (12:16, 23) and calls for the sacrificial blood to be poured on the altar (12:27). Moreover, Von Rad[51] sees a hint of the idea of expiation through the vicarious death of the animal in Deut. 21:8. But it appears to me that the Deuteronomist stops short of attributing atoning power to the sacrificial blood. Deut. 21:9 implies that the really effective factor is not the sacrificial animal but Israel's obedience. Ordinarily sacrifice in Deuteronomy is an occasion for rejoicing (12:11–12; 12:18; 27:7) rather than a means of atonement.

As suggested before, one way of maintaining life in the land in Deuteronomy is obedience. If Israel is obedient, she will live and be secure (8:1; 11:26–28; 6:18; 7:12; 16:20; 4:1, 5). On the other hand, it is a strong theme in Deuteronomy that God loves Israel and chooses her without regard for her merit (7:7–8; 10:15; 8:17; 9:4). God goes before Israel and fights for her (1:30–32). He has acted in history on Israel's behalf; therefore, Israel's obedience is an appropriate response (5:6–21; 6:20–25; 7:6; 14:1–2; 8:4; 26:5–11; 27:9–10) and not a condition for obtaining life and escaping death. Von Rad wants to see the latter of these two ways of salvation as dominant and as in accord with the New Testament, while he takes the former motif to be minor.[52] But I think that we must simply concede that we have a clear opposition between two ways of mediating between death and life: the obedience of Israel/ the historical action of God. But more needs to be said about how Deuteronomy understands God's historical act and how the latter mediates between life and death.

God's action in Deuteronomy is life-giving, as we have seen. His word also is life (8:3), and particularly is the efficaciousness of the word suggested by the Song of Moses (31:30–32:2). Thus God's life-giving action seems to be interpreted in Deuteronomy as his life-giving word. This understanding of the matter is confirmed by the fact that Moses, who has been the instrument of God's action, will be replaced after his death by his word, which will continue to encounter Israel (31:28–29). Moses was the most extraordinarily powerful of all the prophets (34:10–12), but he will be followed by another prophet like him in whom his word will continue to speak itself (18:15, 18).

The word is the power of life because its content is life: its proclamation is able to evoke and qualify life because it proclaims God's life-giving power. It is able to mediate between death and life because it (the word *word*) means both law (4:2, 10; 11:18; 17:19; 28:14) and kerygma (1:30–32; 5:5–6; 31:30ff.). The latter is seen especially in the Song of Moses. First Yahweh's creative care and action for Israel are proclaimed (32:6–13) and then Israel's thankless rebellion is remembered (32:15–18). In consequence God executed his destructive judgment (32:19–35) upon Israel. This can also be expressed in terms of the word as law. When the word of law is not interiorized and obeyed (cf. 30:14 with 32:46) it produces death (11:13–28). Thus we see that the word of life (kerygma) includes within itself the word of death (law), and word thus mediates between death and life. The people killed by the disobeyed law are restored to life. To return to the Song of Moses: When God sees that Israel's rebellious power is exhausted he will turn to Israel in compassion and restore her (32:36–43). As a result the opposition give life/kill (32:6–13/32:19–35) is transformed into the opposition kill/make alive (32:19–35/ 32:36–43), for Yahweh is the God who kills to make alive (32:39). (Note the relationship to the structure of Hosea in figure #6). And the word of the Song of Moses is seen to be a word of death and resurrection.

Now Paul would not have been attracted to the theme of salvation by obedience (works) in either Leviticus or Deuteronomy, and the motif of the atoning sacrificial blood has little place in Paul's theology.[53] But Paul would have had a natural affinity—conscious, unconscious, or partly both—with the theology of the word in Deuteronomy. This was structurally related to his own thought; therefore, he saw his theology expressed in Deuteronomy. Recall that in Deuteronomy word means both law and kerygmatic saving event, while in Paul it means simply the latter. As a result he tended to see it as always meaning kerygma in Deuteronomy. Consequently he read word in Deut. 30:14 to mean kerygma when it actually meant law (see Deut. 30:11). Therefore, Paul misinterpreted Deut. 30:11–14, but his global understanding of Deuteronomy is correct. Not only does Deuteronomy have the theology of the word but the syntagm of Deuteronomy is seen to be a transformation in the genre-structure which we have been developing (see figure #6). Notice especially that in Paul we have the death of Jesus and his resurrection-word which shatters man in order to save him, while in Deuteronomy we have the death of Moses, who is also "resurrected" into his word, which kills in order to make alive. We do not suggest that Paul thought consciously of these parallels, but he was led to see his theology in Deuteronomy because his thought and Deuteronomy belonged to what Michel Foucault would call the same *episteme* or epistemological field: that unconscious order, arrangement, or configuration of ideas and discourse in which a culture feels at home, that kind of rationality by which a culture seeks to constitute the knowledge of something as knowledge.[54]

In the light of the foregoing it cannot be said, as Bultmann does say, that the faith of the New Testament was worked out quite independently of the Old Testament. Bultmann's grounding for this position is that the New Testament—through the use of allegory—reads meanings into the Old Testament which the latter cannot bear in its own historical setting. That proves that the New Testament stood firm on its own feet and only later used the Old Testament as a means for expressing its own, previously developed and independently worked-out faith. Bultmann's basic presupposition for all of this is that the *only* evidence for assessing the relationship between the Old Testament and the New is that which can be established by historical research.[55]

Paul sometimes did allegorize in details, but the historical approach is *not* the only one to theological questions in the Bible. Structural analysis has shown that Paul understood Deuteronomy at the global level. Paul works within a meaning-system, a structure, within which Deuteronomy is also a transformation. The structural system in conjunction with Paul's experience of and reflection on the Christian kerygma produced Paul's theology, and Paul in turn as a Christian theologian over-Christianizes parts of the system which had helped to confer his theological position upon him. But at least there is interaction between Paul and the larger structure. Thus we must consider the possibility that Paul could see the resurrection of Jesus as word or kerygma, not just because of his and the church's encounter with the word, but also because of what Deuteronomy contributed to the resurrection paradigm. Deuteronomy is significant for Paul's theology, not just because the book belonged to Paul's historical tradition and may have influenced him in a direct, conscious, and historical way, but because both some of Paul's texts and Deuteronomy are generated by the same genre. Deuteronomy is, therefore, a clue to the genre which unconsciously produced the Pauline performance texts (texts actually uttered) in question. Or we could say that Paul was consciously drawn to a particular item in his historical tradition—Deuteronomy—because both Deuteronomy and the shape of Paul's own theological expression were already generated by the same genre-structure.

Now we can see why—although Käsemann does not explain it— Paul's concept of justification by faith led him to see the near word of justification in Deuteronomy. Both Paul's kerygma of the death and resurrection of Jesus (justification by faith) and the content of the word in Deuteronomy have God bringing life out of death: God kills to make alive; he shatters the boastful wisdom and righteousness of man in order to give justification, life, and true wisdom.

The cross and resurrection of Jesus generated for Paul a new perspective into which he took old terms (like "justification," "righteousness," and "near word") but the very fact that he retains some of the old terms facilitated the transformations within the system.

The old terms are given new meanings within Paul's kerygma, but they *are* retained and do not lose all of their old significance. This demonstrates the openness of the old texts and the polysemous nature of their words.[56] On the assumption that Paul's audience put some stock in the Old Testament, we may affirm that the apostle was intuitively following the rule of compatibility: no proclamation will reach anyone if it cannot make some contact with the hearer's preunderstanding. The new meaning system cannot be too incompatible with the hearer's frame of reference.[57] Paul's new message makes contact with a context provided by an item in his hearer's historical tradition—Deuteronomy—and also by the comic genre, which is a structure of the human mind.

The eschatological Christ event was of crucial importance for Paul's new way of knowing.[58] In emphasizing this point J. Louis Martyn is concerned with Paul's negative relationship to Corinthian gnosticism while I am here concerned with his positive relationship to Deuteronomy. But he raises, at least implicitly, some of the same questions. By stressing the importance of the eschatological turning of the ages in Christ, Martyn may not be allowing, however, sufficient place for its interaction with the structure or meaning-system with which Paul worked.

But Martyn's point that Paul was determined to live in the cross, and not before or after it, like his Corinthian opponents,[59] is a good one. This means that for Paul the Christian sees partially, sees the new hidden in the old, the resurrection in the cross. He does not see—as the gnostic thinks he does—without hindrance.[60]

This leads me to a final note. While the Pauline Christian does not claim that radical, undialectical newness which the gnostic claims, there is a sense in which Paul's understanding of renewal—living in the cross *and* resurrection—is more radical than the gnostic conception of salvation.

For the gnostic, knowledge brings out what is naturally, if latently, already there. Man knows himself in relation to God and the universe and has his true self realized by the actualization of the divine self which was naturally there within him though hidden.

For Paul man must *choose* (Rom. 13:14; Phil. 2:5)—to know himself in the paradigm of the cross and resurrection (Gal. 2:20;

Rom. 6:5–6) of Jesus, and by so doing—and also by a gift—he becomes something else, even if he is only on the way. The Pauline Christian does not know himself in relation to God and the world by having what he already latently knows brought to light, but by choosing a paradigm which comes to him out of his trans-personal history as a model for his life. Thus he knows and becomes himself by deciding for a model outside of himself. (The comic structure as a human rhythm *is* a point of contact for this decision.) He does not merely bring the latent to light. He does not claim the freedom from the world which the gnostic claims, but he is more radically new. He does not just realize what he naturally is but moves out of the wrath of God (Romans 1–2) and the old eon (Romans 5) into a new creation (2 Cor. 5:17). He is still dialectically in the old, but so far as he is new, his newness is more radically conceived than is the case in gnosticism.

Yet the newly created self of the Pauline man of faith retains its own individuality whether that individual selfhood be thought of under the aspect of his "I" (1 Cor. 15:10; Gal. 2:20), his mind, or inward man (Rom. 7:22–23; 2 Cor. 4:16), his spirit (1 Cor. 2:11; Rom. 8:16), his flesh (Gal. 2:20), or his body (2 Cor. 4:7, 10; Rom. 8:11). In summary: The new self of the gnostic is the divine fragment awakened to an efficacious knowledge of its ontological identity with the divine. The new self of the Pauline Christian does not lose its irreducible individuality, but that individuality is projected into the paradigm of the death and resurrection of Jesus, the story of which is continuous with other comic syntagms and puts the man of Christian faith in touch with all those comic possibilities by the reverberations which it sets up.

NOTES TO CHAPTER II

1. Werner Kramer, *Christ, Lord, Son of God*, trans. B. Hardy (London: SCM Press, 1966), pp. 20, 30, 33, 34.
2. Ibid., pp. 26–28.
3. Ibid., pp. 32, 33, 36.
4. Ibid., pp. 28, 30, 32, 119.
5. A. J. Greimas, "Structure et Histoire," *Les Temps Modernes* 22, no. 246 (1966): 825–827.
6. See Paul Ricoeur, *De l'interprétation* (Paris: Editions du Seuil, 1965), pp. 47–48.
7. See Claude Lévi-Strauss, *The Savage Mind* (Chicago: University of Chicago Press, 1970), pp. 65–66, 139, 161, 263–264, 267–268; *The Raw and the Cooked*, trans. J. and D. Weightman, (New York: Harper & Row, 1970), pp. 10–13, 341. See also Paul Ricoeur, "Structure et herméneutique," *Esprit* (nouvelle série), no. 322 (November, 1963): 601, 605: C. Chabrol, "Problèmes de la sémiotique narrative des récits bibliques," *Langages* 6, no. 22 (June, 1971): 5, 9; Edmund Leach, "The Legitimacy of Solomon: Some Structural Aspects of Old Testament History," *European Journal of Sociology* 7, no. 1 (1966): 63, 80–81; Jean Piaget, *Structuralism*, trans. C. Maschler (New York: Basic Books, 1970), p. 76; G. Schiwy, *Neue Aspekte des Strukturalismus* (München: Kösel Verlag, 1971), pp. 174–176. One is, therefore, for all these reasons inclined to disagree with the insistence of Käsemann that the cross is the center of Paul's theology. Käsemann will not concede that the cross is one of several key themes or that the center is a double focus on the cross and resurrection. Yet Käsemann can also say that for Paul cross and resurrection count as a single event. See Ernst Käsemann, *Perspectives on Paul*, trans. M. Kohl (Philadelphia: Fortress Press, 1971), pp. 46–48, 95.
8. See Hans Conzelmann, *Der erste Brief an die Korinther* (Göttingen: Vandenhoeck und Ruprecht, 1969), p. 53. Wilhelm Wuellner also makes an attempt to establish the unity of 1 Cor. 1–3 and to explain certain other problems by positing behind 1 Cor. 1–3 a Jewish homily pattern which may be seen reflected also in other New Testament texts. See Wilhelm Wuellner, "Haggadic Homily Genre in 1 Corinthians 1–3," *Journal of Biblical Literature* 89, part 2 (June, 1970): 199–204.
9. Conzelmann, *Der erste Brief*, p. 62.
10. See Emile Benveniste, *Problèmes de linguistique générale* (Paris: Editions Gallimard, 1966), pp. 233, 235.
11. See Wylie Sypher, "The Meanings of Comedy," p. 26; Susanne Langer, "The Comic Rhythm," pp. 126, 137; L. C. Knights, "Notes on Comedy," pp. 181–182; J. T. Styan, "Types of Comedy," p. 234; all in Robert W. Corrigan, *Comedy* (San Francisco: Chandler Publishing Co., 1965).
12. See Francis M. Cornford, *The Origin of Attic Comedy* (Cambridge: Cambridge University Press, 1934), p. 199.
13. Conzelmann, *Der erste Brief*, pp. 52, 55, 70.
14. Benveniste, *Problèmes*, pp. 228, 252–253.
15. See Geoffrey Hartman, "Structuralism: The Anglo-American Adventure," in *Structuralism, Yale French Studies* 36 and 37 (1966): 151–152.

16. Cornford, *Attic Comedy*, pp. vii, 3–4, 18–21, 24–25, 51–59, 60, 68, 113, 208, 212. For more recent confirmation of these themes in ancient Greek religion see A. W. H. Adkins, "Greek Religion," in *Historia Religionum*, ed. C. J. Bleeker and G. Widengren (Leiden: E. J. Brill, 1969), pp. 385–386, 397–398, 416; Martin P. Nilsson, *A History of Greek Religion*, trans. F. J. Fielden (2d rev ed., 1952; New York: W. W. Norton and Co., 1964), pp. 91, 95, 96–99, 107, 108, 117, 121.

17. See Sypher, pp. 33–34 and Langer, p. 124, in Corrigan, *Comedy*; Moses Hadas, "Introduction," *The Complete Plays of Aristophanes* (New York: Bantam Books, 1971), p. 6.

18. Cornford, *Attic Comedy,* pp. 2, 3, 8, 24, 71, 85–93, 171. Sypher, again, supports this view in Corrigan, *Comedy*, pp. 34–35.

19. Cornford, *Attic Comedy*, pp. 71, 136–139; Sypher, in Corrigan, *Comedy*, pp. 41–42.

20. Cornford, *Attic Comedy*, pp. 132, 136–138, 140, 148, 156.

21. Ibid., pp. 18–20.

22. See Benjamin Lehmann, "Comedy and Laughter," in Corrigan, *Comedy*, p. 164.

23. Sypher, in Corrigan, *Comedy*, pp. 37, 50.

24. Robert W. Corrigan, "Comedy and the Comic Spirit," in Corrigan, *Comedy*, p. 3.

25. Sypher, in Corrigan, *Comedy,* pp. 20, 36–37.

26. Harold H. Watts, "The Sense of Regain: A Theory of Comedy," in Corrigan, *Comedy*, pp. 194, 197.

27. Langer, in Corrigan, *Comedy*, pp. 123–124.

28. See Ludwig Jekels, "On the Psychology of Comedy," pp. 264, 267–268 and Martin Grotjahn, "Beyond Laughter: A Summing Up," p. 273 in Corrigan, *Comedy*.

29. Langer, in Corrigan, *Comedy*, p. 126.

30. See Gaston Bachelard, *The Poetics of Space*, trans. M. Jolas (New York: Orion Press, 1964), pp. xii–xix, xxiii, xxvi, 32; Sypher, in Corrigan, *Comedy*, p. 23.

31. See Cornford, *Attic Comedy*, pp. viii, 212; Sypher, p. 18 and Jekels, pp. 267–268 in Corrigan, *Comedy*.

32. Claude Bremond, "La logique des possibles narratifs," *Communications* 8 (1966): 60–62.

33. See Käsemann, *Paul*, pp. 146–147, 151, 155.

34. Ibid., p. 155.

35. Ibid., pp. 158–159, 164–166.

36. This is the meaning which Käsemann assigns to spirit in primitive Christianity. See *ibid.*, p. 139.

37. This discussion of the structure of signification and the component factors is based on A. J. Greimas, *Sémantique Structurale* (Paris: Librairie Larousse, 1966), pp. 19–32, 34, 38; Schiwy, *Neue Aspekte*, pp. 174–175.

38. See Eberhard Jüngel, *Paulus und Jesus* (Tübingen: J. C. B. Mohr, 1967), p. 61.

39. For a fuller defense of this point see Dan O. Via, Jr., "The Right Strawy Epistle Reconsidered," *The Journal of Religion* 49, no. 3 (1969): 257–258.

40. See M. Jack Suggs, " 'The Word Is near You': Romans 10:6–10 within

the Purpose of the Letter," in *Christian History and Interpretation*, ed. W. R. Farmer, C. F. D. Moule, R. R. Niebuhr (Cambridge: Cambridge University Press, 1967), p. 301.

41. See Käsemann, *Paul*, p. 79.

42. Bornkamm also compares the faith of Abraham to that of the Christian. See Günther Bornkamm, *Paul*, trans. D. M. G. Stalker (New York and Evanston: Harper & Row, 1969), p. 144.

43. See Jüngel, *Paulus und Jesus*, pp. 46–47; Käsemann, *Paul*, pp. 40, 90, 92.

44. Notice the opposite terminology of the resurrection situation used in Romans 4—calling into existence that which is not.

45. Käsemann, *Paul*, p. 88.

46. Suggs, " 'The Word Is near You,' " p. 304.

47. Ibid., pp. 308–310; according to Käseman (*Paul*, p. 160), this ascending-descending terminology was simply a way of describing a superhuman effort toward some impossible goal.

48. Suggs, " 'The World Is near You,' " pp. 310–311.

49. Edmund Leach has shown that, in certain strands in the Old Testament, thought does operate as mediation between oppositions ("The Legitimacy of Solomon," pp. 63–64).

50. Gerhard von Rad, *Old Testament Theology*, I, trans. D. M. G. Stalker (Edinburgh and London: Oliver and Boyd, 1962), pp. 251, 260, 270.

51. Ibid., p. 270.

52. Ibid., pp. 229–231.

53. It appears occasionally (as in Rom. 3:25; 1 Cor. 10:16; 11:25), perhaps influenced primarily by pre-Pauline formulas. The significance of Jesus' death is usually interpreted in categories other than sacrificial blood. See Käsemann, *Paul*, pp. 40, 43.

54. See Michel Foucault, *The Order of Things*, trans. not indicated (New York: Random House, Pantheon Books, 1970), pp. xi, xx, xxii, 157, 200, 356.

55. Rudolf Bultmann, "The Significance of the Old Testament for the Christian Faith," trans. B. W. Anderson, in B. W. Anderson, *The Old Testament and Christian Faith* (New York: Harper & Row, 1963), pp. 32–33.

56. See C. Chabrol; "Analyse du 'texte' de la Passion," *Langages* 6, no. 22 (June, 1971): 91–92.

57. See Schiwy, *Neue Aspekte*, p. 180.

58. J. Louis Martyn, "Epistemology at the Turn of the Ages: 2 Cor. 5:16," in *Christian History and Interpretation*, ed. Farmer, Moule, and Niebuhr, pp. 271–275.

59. Ibid., pp. 285–286.

60. Ibid., p. 286.

III

Approaching the
Gospel of Mark

In this chapter I want to take up at greater length an item briefly alluded to in Chapter I—the irony that redaction criticism has turned out to be so historical a discipline. Then I wish to pursue in two parts a question which will open out onto two, or more, other questions. The root question is simply "Why was Mark written in the form in which it was written?" Or if that approaches too closely the intentional fallacy—the false belief that we can ascertain the subjective intention lying behind an author's work, especially in the circumstances of his life—let the question be rather "What in fact did Mark's way of doing his job accomplish?"

A. Contemporary Interpretations of Mark: A Structuralist Critique of Redaction Criticism

What can structuralist analysis say to redaction criticism? A number of the remarks here would apply to the redaction criticism of any of the Gospels, but I will stick to Mark as my example.

C. Chabrol, who practices structuralist criticism on biblical narratives, states that redaction criticism is not structuralist criticism. He says that redaction criticism really belongs to the realm of historical scholarship.[1] Roland Frye, who is not a structuralist but is an eminent American literary critic and also knowledgeable in biblical studies, implies that competent literary critics would not recognize redaction criticism as any kind of literary criticism at all.[2]

Your response may be "so what?" You may say that I am arguing only at the level of epithets and/or that the redaction criticism of the Synoptics *should* be a historical enterprise. I would rejoin that there are substantive issues beneath the epithets and that real benefits would accrue to redaction criticism by making it more literary. Probably no criticism of the New Testament—including redaction criticism—can be purely historical or purely literary. But every New Testament scholar should decide, for the sake of consistency in his work, whether he is going to approach the problems of New Testament interpretation *primarily* as a historical critic or as a literary critic. Or at least he should be aware of which option he has chosen for a given study.

What is the main substantive issue involved in the conflict between literary and redaction criticism? Several years ago it was difficult for me to make a clear distinction between the literary and redaction criticism of the Gospels: the two tended to coalesce in my mind. But now the distinction seems very clear. Literary criticism seeks to apprehend a text as a whole or a totality,[3] and that includes structuralist criticism,[4] although as we have often seen the latter also wants to do more. From Marxsen up to the most recent times, however, redaction critics (or composition critics or "Gattung critics") have split Mark into tradition (sources) and redaction and have sought to establish chronological-genetic-causal relations between these two strata.[5] Or they have supposed that in order to understand Mark we must know the model or the ingredients to which Mark can be genetically related or from which the Gospel emerged.[6] This splitting of Mark into tradition and redaction is not accidental to the redaction-critical method but is a matter of principle. Leander Keck states that the differences between tradition and redaction must be allowed to stand in their tension.[7] Those who practice this kind of criticism are known in English literary circles as "disintegrators."[8]

In a given redaction-critical study the tradition is usually forgotten as soon as it and the redaction have been distinguished, and the real interest is seen to be the theology of Mark, the author, as differentiated from the tradition which he used. As provocative and interesting as these studies often are for historical purposes, the text as a whole, as a narrative, in the form in which it confronts the reader and needs explication, is lost sight of. Mark—or the author's theology, for the Gospel as a narrative whole is ignored— is seen as the product of a source, the modification of a model, the effect of a cause (the cause being, for example, a heresy in Mark's church and/or the sources expressing the heresy) and not as the signifier of a signified (its genre). In treating Mark as the product of a source redaction criticism falls under both of the charges which Roland Barthes brings against that view of a text. It says too little because it leaves the source behind and does not grasp the whole. But this is preceded by an attempt at too much, namely, the effort to make distinctions and show connections where the evidence is insufficient. Perhaps it should be pointed out that, when structuralist criticism decomposes a narrative, it does not make a separation between sources and the author's contribution; it is not a separation between materials historically distinct. Rather it is an effort to grasp the logic of the narrative as a whole or the logic of the fundamental sequences, which may be a clue to the former.

Let us look at one concrete example of redaction criticism's failure to grasp the narrative as a whole, or in this particular case, a failure to grasp a unity within the Gospel of Mark. This failure is grounded in the distinction between tradition and redaction, and it really represents a failure to see the simple fact of how people read narratives. Georg Strecker states that Mark (like the other Synoptic Evangelists) is interested, not in the atoning significance of Jesus' death, but in the fact of it. If one wants to find Jesus' death interpreted as atoning in Mark, one must look to pre-redactional elements (like 14:24).[9] Thus in true redaction-critical fashion Strecker separates fact from interpretation, sets them over against each other as unrelated, and attributes them to two different theologies—all of this, incredibly, despite the fact that both belong to the same *story*. Strecker's presentation gives us a clear case of historical criticism's victory over literary criticism and the consequent distorting of the nature and meaning of the text being interpreted—that is, the Gospel of Mark. Strecker logically would handle Mark 10:45 in the same way, *if* he took this verse to present Jesus' death as atoning, but he rather takes it—wrongly in my judgment—to present Jesus' death simply as exemplary.[10]

But let us assume, at least for the sake of argument, that H. E.

Tödt is right in understanding Mark 10:45 as being pre-Markan tradition and as interpreting Jesus' service as a once-for-all giving of his life as a ransom for the many.[11] How would structuralist criticism treat the relationship between Mark 10:45 and the passion narrative as composed by Mark? In the first place it would not be too interested in the fact that at some stage Mark 10:45 and the passion narrative were separate elements. Structural analysis will recognize the verse as belonging to both the discourse and story levels of Mark (see Chapter IV for a further discussion of these two narrative levels). As discourse 10:45 is a part of the message which the narrator is speaking to his audience. As story it is an action of Jesus—a statement—and functions in at least two ways. It is the acceptance of the implied contractual mandate (from God) assumed in the notion that the Son of Man must suffer (8:31).[12] Also because Jesus' word is effective in Mark the statement has a causal relationship to the passion narrative. It is a seed which will ripen at another point:[13] as the sown seed which ripens in the death of Jesus this spoken word has both a syntactic and a semantic relationship to the passion narrative and contributes to the latter in terms of both causality and significance.

While Theodore Weeden's provocative book is more circumspect than some other studies in its acknowledgment of the difficulty often attendant upon trying to distinguish tradition from redaction, he still treats Mark as the product of a source—a heretical threat in Mark's church and the oral or written sources representing it.[14] According to Weeden, Mark has Jesus' disciples represent the heretics, and Weeden ascribes to Mark's "stroke of genius" the plan of dramatizing the christological debate in Mark's church through the relationship between Jesus and his disciples.[15] It is interesting to juxtapose this formulation with Roland Barthes's observation that those critics who treat a text as the product of a source typically attribute the difference which the author makes in his sources to "genius."[16]

Weeden's hermeneutical approach to Mark is both historical and literary. He wants to read Mark with first-century eyes, but he wants to see it as a Greco-Roman would have seen a *literary* work. Hellenistic education believed that a reader understood a work and judged its import through the characters and the events in which they were involved.[17] Weeden makes an interesting case, and the approach is valid, if partial, but the particular way in which Weeden employs this method leads him to a strange anomaly.

If Mark wanted to make his point and win his readers to faith in Jesus by his treatment of the characters, and if the relationship between Jesus and his disciples is as Weeden depicts it, then Mark seems to have bungled the job. In Weeden's opinion the disciples hardly have any awareness of who Jesus is in Mark 1:16–8:26; then at Caesarea-Philippi they mistakenly recognize him as a divine man messiah; and finally they reject him altogether.[18] Now the strange thing is that this view of the course of events turns Jesus himself into a rather reprehensible character. In the first part of Mark Jesus performs many miracles in the presence of his disciples (a primary divine man function), and Weeden himself says that if we only had Mark 1:1–8:29 we would have to conclude that Mark also interpreted Jesus' messiahship in divine man terms.[19] Thus how can the disciples be blamed for coming to the conclusion that Jesus is a divine man? Hence it turns out that according to Weeden's interpretation the disciples are utterly and finally repudiated by Jesus[20] because they are never able to get over a false christological faith into which Jesus himself has led them. True they received instruction in suffering messiahship in the second half of the book, but the fact remains that in Weeden's view, inescapably, it is Jesus' own activity that induces in them the wrong Christology to begin with.

The Markan Jesus would be let off the hook somewhat if we recognize with Keck that there are two miracle traditions in the first part of Mark. Jesus is not wholly the Hellenistic "divine man." He is also the Palestinian eschatological "strong man."[21] That would make the critique of the disciples more plausible.

But a part of Weeden's problem is also the hermeneutical *choice* to attempt to stick close to the first century and to force the disciples into the role of representing Mark's opponents (a role for which he gives very little evidence). Perhaps we need a less restricted signified for our signifier (the relation between Jesus and the disciples). Maybe the disciples do not so much—or at least so exclusively—reflect the historical problem of Mark's opponents as the existential problem of the difficulty of man's grasping the revelation of God in a suffering messiah, the difficulty of appropriating existentially what one has been instructed about intellectually. This also is a chosen signified or point of pertinence, but it can make some claim to account for the phenomena in the Gospel without making Jesus look so bad, or Mark's narrative logic look so unconvincing.

In his recent book on form criticism Erhardt Güttgemanns states that his basic goal is to revise the methodological framework of form and redaction criticism by using certain insights from linguistics and literary scholarship. He calls explicitly for a structural analysis of the Gospel of Mark.[22] Let us consider his main points and see what fruit they bear.

Güttgemanns attacks the view that the Gospel form emerged continuously out of earlier oral tradition.[23] We have the Gospel (Mark as the earliest in his view) and its materials only in written form and no direct access to the oral tradition and its processes. Thus there is no empirical evidence for the laws that governed the oral stage; therefore we cannot say that the written stage is governed by the same laws or the written Gospel emerged according to them.[24] Somewhat more theoretically he points out that the written stage provides a new framework and principle of organization for the individual pieces. Writing itself introduces changes; it fixes speech spatially and allows new possibilities such as turning back pages and repetition. The new framework creates a gestalt, a whole which is more than the sum of its parts and cannot be genetically derived from them.[25]

Güttgemanns, of course, does not deny that Mark used earlier materials, but asserts that we cannot pierce through the compactness of the Markan composition sufficiently well to make clear distinctions. The Gospel is Mark's creative literary act, and we must concern ourselves with an intra-Markan structural analysis.[26]

What was the organizing principle for the new gestalt? Was it the kerygma? For Güttgemanns the answer is "no." We are really not certain whether the Synoptic tradition or the kerygma developed earlier. Beyond that, the kerygma as we have it in the New Testament lacks unity and if there was an original, comprehensive credo, it has virtually disappeared into the primitive Christian darkness. Therefore, we cannot show that the Gospel is an expan-

sion of the kerygma. We can say that in Mark a theologically significant content has acquired a gestalt. The Gospel is "auto-
semantic," meaningful in itself.[27]

Güttgemanns denies the judgment of Dibelius, Weiss, and others
that the Synoptic tradition illustrates the bare, nonconcrete
kerygma.[28] Instead of staying, however, with this question, the
question which he explicitly raised, he moves into a denial of the
contention that the *vividness* of the Synoptic narrative is an inherent proof of its own historicity,[29] which is quite another problem. To show that the vividness of Mark—or any other narrative—
is the vividness of poetry and not a proof of the historicity of the
narrative, however, is not to disprove, or even to touch on the
question, whether the Synoptic tradition illustrates or gives vividness to the kerygma—or to *some* kerygma.

Güttgemanns's argument that Mark should be treated as a whole
and viewed in itself is well taken. It receives support from Polanyi's
argument that the highest level of a comprehensive entity cannot
be governed by the laws of the lower levels. It is possible for man
to create a gestalt because the mind or psyche is a gestalt,[30] or better, the body-self which unites subject and object within itself is a
gestalt.[31] This gestalt-self overcomes the bifurcation between object
(source) and subject (creative input of author) and renders a
unified work.

I agree with Güttgemanns's playing down of the genetic connections between sources and finished Gospel, but structural analysis may be able to show some generic kinship between the Gospel
and some of its unit-sequences.

Güttgemanns is probably right in discounting the possibility of
tracing a diachronic connection between the kerygma and the
Gospel. But there are other matters to be considered. There is a
probable tendency toward narration in the Pauline death-resurrection kerygma, because, as Ricoeur has shown, a symbol tends to
place itself in a larger meaningful totality.[32] There is a structural
(synchronic) relationship between Paul's kerygma and the Gospel
of Mark because these two belong, together with the plays of
Aristophanes and the ancient Greek death-resurrection ritual, to
the same genre. Nor is Güttgemanns correct, I think, in holding
that Mark 8:31; 9:31; 10:33–34 summarize Mark only from 8:27

to the end.[33] These passages express the death-resurrection motif which lies at the heart of the comic structure, and structural analysis will show that the *whole* of Mark is a transformation within that structure.

Güttgemanns's position is superior to that of current redaction criticism in that he sees the Gospel as a gestalt which must be grasped as a whole. However, he leaves the door open theoretically for Mark's organic integrity to be cracked. Güttgemanns thinks of Mark as a creative author with a certain intention working in a particular historical situation.[34] But a historical, creative author makes a work out of something; therefore, the concept of the work as a product is lurking in the shadows. The concept of the historical author and that of the work as a product go together while the concept of the "incarnate author" or narrator and that of the work as a signifier go together.

Once a work is written it is detached from its historical author. The real concern of criticism—for many structuralists and critics of consciousness—is the narrator. He is not the one who writes the text but is the new implied being who assumes form as the work is being created.[35] He is the one who expresses the *valuational* element which is inherent in the book, a valuation which is a part neither of the experience of the reader nor of the historical author.[36] Perhaps we could say that the narrator is an aspect of the author, a position supported by the idea that a writer thinks with his materials, not with ideas that he imposes upon them.[37] Since the creation of the literary work and thought occur simultaneously, the narrator is the author as he is in and for the work and not as he is in his own historical situation. Thus the narrator is understood as a figure created, at least in part, by the materials-in-the-process-of-becoming-a-work, and he in turn confers on the work a unity. This curtails the possibility of considering the work as a product made by an author and opens up the way of seeing it as a signifier. New Testament scholarship might consider the applicability of the concept of the narrator or "incarnate author."

B. Apocalyptic and the Gospel of Mark

When the question is raised implicitly or explicitly—why was Mark written in this particular form?—usually two related answers are given: (1) it was written to express a certain meaning or concept; (2) it was written to meet a particular historical situation. The factor of meaning raises the question of genre since the genre of a text is a clue to the meaning of the text.[38] Therefore, I am devoting a section to apocalyptic: because it has recently been suggested that apocalyptic is the genre of Mark, because apocalyptic is a prominent theme in the New Testament and its milieu and also expresses itself in various modern forms, because this discussion will allow me to take up again the question of the relationship of Mark to the kerygma: "Jesus died and rose again" (1 Thess. 4:14) is a compact apocalypse—of a certain kind.

Norman Perrin argues that Mark was creating a new genre, but he also suggests that in doing so Mark was following the apocalyptic model.[39] Elsewhere Perrin states that Mark in many respects is "essentially an apocalypse." He does not mention many respects other than Mark's expectation of the imminent parousia and his view of a single, unified history which leads from John the Baptist into the reader's own time.[40] This line of argument implies that Mark's genre is a transformation within the genre apocalypse. Werner Kelber[41] makes the bold statement that Mark is "an apocalyptic vision." To be sure other scholars have pointed out additional apocalyptic features and have argued for Mark's apocalyptic nature—the theme of the fulfillment of prediction, the element of divine necessity, the resurrection, signs of the end, the bleakness of history after Easter, the great tribulation, etc.[42] But are these undeniably apocalyptic features sufficient to make Mark a representative of the apocalyptic genre? I will argue in various ways that they are not.

Perrin himself contends that there is a certain instability about Mark—a conflict between its realistic narrative form and its apocalyptic purpose. Yet Perrin refers to both the apocalyptic element and the realistic features as serving to engage the reader in the narrative.[43] This common function tends to moderate the alleged instability or conflict, which is not a conflict at all but rather a matter of the relationship and synthesis between two narrative levels—the symbolic and the representational—which characteristically belong to any narrative, although the two levels may be present in different narratives in varying degrees and synthesized in diverse ways.[44] This question of narrative levels will be discussed at length in Chapter IV.

Perrin also gives a historical answer to the question about why Mark was written: to correct a false divine man Christology which existed in Mark's church.[45] Perrin does not clarify precisely how Mark's combination of apocalyptic and realism is supposed to counter this particular heresy, but probably could do so.

At this stage I should like to give a more complete description of apocalyptic and then to test in a provisional way Mark's generic status against this presentation. With regard to literary forms apocalyptic is characterized by pseudonymity, symbolism which tends toward the fantastic and bizarre, surveys of history in future form, predictions about and descriptions of the world to come typically in the form of dreams, visions, ecstasies, trances, heavenly journeys, and angelic messages. However, occasionally the visionary form is replaced by that of the farewell discourse. As for the two primary biblical apocalypses, in Daniel, dreams, visions, and surveys of history in future form are prominent, while Revelation is as a whole the record of a vision.[46]

With respect to its concepts apocalyptic may be summarized in the following way: (1) History receives a very negative evaluation. Under demonic control and deteriorating in quality, what can happen in the historical process and the number and length of its periods have been determined in advance. (2) History as such will be dissolved and judged in the near future. (3) A new world wholly unlike this one will be introduced by God "from beyond."[47]

Despite this negative evaluation of history Rowley and Russell see in apocalyptic something akin to the prophetic salvation history in which God is understood as active in the affairs of men.[48] Klaus Koch accepts the position of the Pannenberg school that apocalyptic is the proper horizon for the whole of Christian theology. His position rests on the claim that apocalyptic developed a total conception of universal history, a history in which God is active and through which he is shaping and reshaping the world.[49]

I am persuaded, however, that for the apocalyptic view God has largely withdrawn from activity in world history and turned the latter over to the Satanic powers. It is also doubtful that the unity of world history is at the center of apocalyptic thinking, but even to the extent that universal history does come into the picture, it is the deteriorating universal history of man.[50] Koch is able to give apocalyptic an affirmative evaluation only by playing down determinism and the dualism between present and future[51] and by ignoring altogether that apocalyptic presents history as a process of increasing deterioration (Dan. 4:31–45; 7:2–12).

Let us now return to the Gospel of Mark. To be sure it has, as we have seen, some apocalyptic elements. But none of the formal qualities which are typical of apocalyptic are really prominent in Mark. Even Mark's most apocalyptic section, chapter 13, takes the form of a farewell discourse rather than the more characteristic revelatory vision of Revelation. Formally Mark is quite atypical of apocalyptic: a unified, connected narrative focusing on a single protagonist, a narrative which has led to the generic comparison of Mark with Greek tragedy, Christian novels, and the dramatic histories of Shakespeare, Shaw, and Robert Sherwood. (This will be further developed in the next section.)

When we turn to the question of thematic content we find that Mark's emphases are different from apocalyptic. Mark expects the judgment of history and the introduction of a new age (8:38–9:1; 10:30; 13:24–27; 12:25), but he does not in characteristic apocalyptic fashion develop these themes with elaborated symbolic detail. As for his view of historical existence itself, it is very remote from that of apocalyptic. In order to grasp the nature of Mark's understanding of historical existence for the man of faith we cannot restrict ourselves to considering only those passages which obviously refer to the span of history between the resurrection and the parousia (13:5–37; 4:14–20). The whole book is Jesus' story, and being a disciple is following in Jesus' way (1:17; 2:13–17; 8:34; 3:13–15). Therefore, Jesus' whole story is the paradigm which gives the clue to the content and quality of existence in history. It would seem that for Mark Jesus was not fully who he was at the beginning of the story, but through a process of salvation history he became the dying-rising-enthroned-saving Son of God–Son of Man (8:31; 10:45; 14:61–62; 15:39).[52] Having achieved life through death himself, Jesus is the one who makes it available to others, and these others (disciples, church) also actualize life through death in an ongoing temporal process. As Mark represents it, the disciples of the earthly Jesus followed him in a spatio-temporal way, and the span of history during which the church lives, between the resurrection and the parousia, is also a real temporal-chronological continuum, the time for the conversion of the gentiles.[53] But the paradigm for the quality of historical existence during this latter period is still Jesus' story, for, as we have seen, the church-disciples are those who follow Jesus, and Mark makes a very close connection between Christology and discipleship (10:43–45). Just how Jesus' existence mediates life through death will be considered further in the next chapter.

But let us look now in a more concrete way at the generalities of the preceding paragraph. Mark's temporal continuum has a beginning point: a new possibility is opened up. This is suggested christologically-mythologically-symbolically in the prologue (1:1– 13). Then in 1:14–15 the Evangelist places in Jesus' mouth what has been called the boldest and most unambiguous affirmation of present fulfillment in the New Testament.[54] The individual who lays hold on this moment of fulfillment enters the kingdom like a child, that is, gets a new beginning (10:15). Subsequent to this new beginning Mark keeps the temporality in movement in a number of ways, a few of which will be mentioned. The polarity between present and future in both The Mustard Seed and The Seed Growing Secretly maintains chronology.[55] Because the fulfillment of prophecy in Jesus (1:2–3, 14–15) is not complete but is rather itself another prophecy calling for future fulfillment (13), history is perpetuated. Jesus encounters human opponents, and the demonic also confronts him in historical occurrences. This opposition ensures the continuation of the narrative, for Jesus and for the church.[56] Mark also assumes that what has been done in the past will be remembered into the human future (14:9).[57] Finally Mark keeps the future open as a hope which has not failed and has not been attained by proclaiming the parousia.[58]

Robert Funk and Philipp Vielhauer argue in similar ways—with regard to the teaching of Jesus—that the juxtaposition or coincidence of apocalyptic imminence and present eschatology has had the effect of bracketing out apocalyptic or canceling out the question of the kingdom's point of time. The kingdom is that reality which occurs surprisingly veiled in the obvious, which comes who knows when as the qualifying of the human situation.[59]

Now since Mark also combines apocalyptic and present eschatology, the same kind of thing can be said in principle for him. But if it be said that Mark brackets out apocalyptic in effect, even while using apocalyptic language to some degree, it cannot be said that Mark rejects the temporality of existence. There is no logical reason why the qualification of existence which comes to expression in Mark's narrative cannot be a determination of existence which allows or even requires temporality for its realization,[60] temporality as a chronological continuum.

What then is the understanding of historical existence which meets us in Mark's narrative? Things happen because Jesus "came out" (1:38) to say and to do. His speech and action create a new present in which man with a carefree lack of anxiety is free to act, to fulfill himself, because he need not worry about realizing the future. That is in God's hands (4:26–29).[61] The dynamism of this situation is so new and vital that the old forms and institutions cannot contain it (2:21–22). To lay hold on this new reality man must be capable of hearing with understanding, and this he will be enabled to do (4:21–25, 33–34).[62] Therefore, he will be freed from the guilt that separates from God (2:1–12), from the demonic power that alienates one from self and society (1:21–28, 32–34; 3:20–27; 5:1–20; 9:17–29), from the old monster chaos symbolized by the sea (4:35–41), and from physical illness and impairment (1:29–31, 32–34, 40–45; 5:21–43; 7:31–37; 8:22–26; 10:46–52). In this new time those cultic formulations are annulled which separate man from man and by which some men try to separate others from God (2:13–17). No longer shall the cult deny to men their everyday needs (2:23–28) or prevent them from doing good to others (3:1–6). There is liberation from a moral standard which proceeds from an external code rather than from the heart (7:1–23); no longer are men required to obey Scripture arbitrarily and without understanding, for Scripture can be interpreted against Scripture (10:2–8). Fasting is turned into feasting and celebration (2:18–19), and all of this provides the context for a new community (1:16–20; 3:13–19; 10:29–30) which takes priority over blood relations (3:31–35); one is even given a "place" in the world, for lands go along with all of those brothers and sisters (10:30).

Yet the accepting of the new time is comprehended under the rubric of life through death (8:34) because such acceptance involves the relinquishing of the old forms of security. The new freedom for life comes through the shattering of familiar securities.

If The Seed Growing Secretly (4:26–29) with its offer of a carefree present is one of the chief clues to the quality of the new time, so, paradoxically, is The Doorkeeper (13:33–37). God's nondemanding gift of freedom is strangely laced with the challenge to be on the watch. A part of the challenge is the requirement to discern between those "christological-existential" situations which really determine the issue of one's existence (13:32–37) and those which only appear to be crucial (13:21–23). The demand to be on the watch may require one to sacrifice some of his freedom. Will fasting sometimes be appropriate (2:20)? Man can expect to suffer for his decision to be a part of the new community (10:30; 13:9–13), and he may be asked to give up all his wealth for the poor (10:17–27) or even to die for his faith (10:38–39). But he who serves and makes himself last rather than first will be first (9:33–35; 10:43–44), for risk is the principle of life (9:43–48). Thus this aspect of the new situation can also be comprehended under the rubric of life through death. To relinquish one's freedom (life) for another (a kind of death) is really to enhance one's freedom: it is finally realizable only as a gift from God, beyond man's capacity—that freedom from the self and for the other which is truly life (10:23–27).

In view of both formal and material considerations it seems the better course not to suggest that Mark is generically akin to apocalypse.

I turn now to the related theme of apocalyptic, gnosticism, and the Gospel of Mark. The form which Christian gnosis usually took was a revelation of the resurrected one. This form owed something to the Gattung identified by James Robinson as "sayings of the wise"—a Gattung composed of a collection of loosely connected short sayings which had a history in the Jewish tradition and was manifested in different versions in Q and in the Gospel of Thomas.

While the Gospel of Thomas presupposes that it is the resurrected one who is speaking, Jesus' death and resurrection never explicitly appear.[63] It has been argued that the sayings Gattung had from its beginning an inherent and incipient gnostic tendency. This is because the Gattung characteristically contained the *idea* of hidden wisdom and because the thematic implication of the *form* was that the *word* had intrinsic authority regardless of its historical context or narrative position.[64]

The form of Christian gnosis also probably owed something to the formal qualities, the "revelation" pattern, of Jewish apocalypses.[65] This probability is strengthened by the fact that in the gnostic Apocalypse of Adam, for example, the revelation of gnosis is combined with the typically apocalyptic periodization of history. Thus we may see in this document an actual example of Jewish apocalyptic shifting into gnosticism.[66]

If apocalyptic forms contributed something to gnosticism, it may well be that the "apocalyptic experience" is another part—but not the whole—of the explanation for the origin of gnosticism. R. M. Grant argues that gnosticism might have arisen in part from the belief that the God of this cosmos, in whom apocalyptic believed, had failed to act. This could lead to an anti-cosmic dualism, a movement of concern from world to self, and a desire to escape from this God-abandoned world to a world beyond, a world whose nature could be understood in the light of apocalyptic. Thus gnosticism would have originated from the failure of the apocalyptic hope while certain ingredients from apocalyptic would have been used to reformulate that hope as gnosticism.[67]

But what explains the move from being a disappointed apocalyptist to being a gnostic or enthusiast or over-realized apocalyptist (terms which will be further developed below)? Perhaps we could say that the temporal dualism of the disappointed apocalyptist would prepare him to accept the metaphysical dualism of gnosticism while his disappointment would incline him to replace a hoped for cosmic revolution with the salvation of his spirit-self. But perhaps the real catalyst—at least as far as Christian gnosticism is concerned—which turned apocalyptic toward gnosticism was the proclamation of the death and resurrection of Jesus. This kerygma, as indicated above, is a compact "realized apocalypse"; it proclaims that the new age is here now, especially when Jesus' resurrection is regarded as in a solidarity with the general resurrection (1 Cor. 15:20–21). In certain circles this might have turned an apocalyptic point of view into over-realized apocalyptic or gnosticism.

Apocalyptic, then, may have been a source of gnosticism. On the other hand, Käsemann sees apocalyptic as being the antidote against gnosticism, or what he calls "enthusiasm," especially at Corinth. According to Käsemann, the Corinthian enthusiasts believed that their baptism had conferred upon them a heavenly spiritual body and had degraded their earthly body to a temporary veil. The enthusiast sees himself as living a heavenly existence, elevated above the unredeemed world of history, freed from inter-human responsibilities and even from sexuality. He has given up every future hope because he believes that he has already realized all that apocalyptic still hopes for. Paul fought this view with a theological position composed of present eschatology and apocalyptic. The latter preserves a future expectation and thus dispels the illusion that one has achieved perfection and escaped the historical world with its futurity and hence temporality.[68] One may doubt Käsemann's contention that apocalyptic is the mother of Christian theology and may feel that his position lacks inner consistency. But his global point that the temporality of existence is basic to the New Testament is difficult to gainsay.

Our discussion has suggested that the apocalyptic configuration was an unstable—or should we say flexible?—one. It could turn itself or be turned in different directions. The subsequent discussion of modern apocalyptic will bear this out, but at this point I must return to Mark.

Robinson and Koester suggest that the inherent gnostic tendency of Q was countered by the narrative-historical form-and-content of Mark.[69] On the other hand, Robinson claims that certain features in the early verses of Mark may be at least partially explained by the gnostic Apocalypse of Adam.[70] It seems to me, however, that the parallels which he points out are too few and nonspecific to make it probable that the Apocalypse of Adam was a model for Mark at all. In any case the Illuminator (redeemer figure) in this Apocalypse does not give, as Jesus does in Mark, the work a narrative unity. Moreover, while the Illuminator makes a descent to the world, the phase of the document which deals with him evidently takes place on a trans-worldly stage.[71] Therefore, this work cannot really explain Mark as a total gestalt.

Mark does not resemble the gnostic Gospels in form or content, and we have seen that the same thing is true of its relationship to apocalypse. Mark—whether or not by intention—opposes gnosticism, and the gnostic germ in apocalypse. If the death-resurrection kerygma is (or may be) a catalyst which inclines apocalyptic toward gnosticism, then Mark is a counter against the catalytic tendency and its result in that the Gospel expands this kerygmatic nucleus into a narrative and gives this kerygma a relatively elaborated representational relation to the world. Mark resists the gnostic propensity in apocalyptic: (1) The strong note of fulfillment overcomes the hopelessness which generates gnosticism out of failed apocalyptic; (2) The unrelinquished temporality, the movement from past through present to future, prevents the over-realized apocalyptic which leads to a gnostic sense of being freed from history.

A consideration of modern apocalypse may help to clarify the meaning possibilities in the apocalyptic configuration. Let us recall that there are three main ingredients: (1) a negative evaluation of history; (2) the expectation of imminent catastrophe; (3) the hope for a new world beyond the destruction. Modern apocalyptic —theological, literary, or in some other form—represents a certain selection from, reinterpretation of, or addition to these themes. Jürgen Moltmann "de-negativizes" present history by the way in which he understands the relationship between the present and the future. In Moltmann's judgment Christianity is eschatology or hope, and that really means apocalyptic, for Moltmann believes that there can be no openness for man apart from a *cosmic* eschatology. This involves a reinterpretation of apocalyptic according to which history is not limited by the structures or boundaries of the cosmos; rather the cosmos is historified, eschatologized, and set in motion. This apocalyptic hope contradicts the present, creating in man an unrest and dissatisfaction with things as they are, a dissatisfaction which bores like a thorn into our unfulfilled present and generates a break-away into the future. This reality becomes history on the move.[72] In Moltmann's reinterpreted apocalyptic there is no tendency to escape from history as in the over-realized apocalyptic (gnosticism or enthusiasm) at Corinth. Instead history becomes an indeterminate series of open possibilities moving into a hopeful future.

When we turn to literary apocalyptic various aspects present themselves to us. We may see a more-or-less chronological story of meaninglessness and a denouement suggesting in some way a cosmic collapse. There is hardly a more striking representative of this than Nathanael West's *The Day of the Locust* (a combination of apocalyptic elements #1 and #2). Or we may view a world of flux and chaos from which order has been banished and in which all values have been inverted—as in John Barth's *The Sot-Weed Factor* or Joseph Heller's *Catch 22*[73] (a kind of perverse synthesis of apocalyptic elements #1 and #3). Again, we may be offered the vision of a grand new world already exploded into existence, a new world either in external reality or in the mind. This belief was entertained by many romantics of the late eighteenth and early nineteenth centuries[74] (an absolutizing of apocalyptic element #3, hence fully realized apocalyptic or gnosticism).

In the view of Nathan Scott modern apocalyptic has a negative, in fact, hopeless, evaluation of history which it usually sees as some form of alienation, and it hopes for a new age typically conceived in terms of inwardness, subjectivity, and a reoriented consciousness (he would include Barth, Heller, and others among the literary apocalyptists). The new apostles of apocalypse have given up on this world[75] and on any kind of comprehensive order.

Perhaps the main tendency at work is a reemergence of the romantic hope of realizing the new world now, and especially through literature. The new apocalyptic myth offers an "open-ended form" as over against the closed plot of the traditional novel. There is no center or thematic given, and in place of the static self there appears "a dynamic structure of interrelationships."[76] For Robbe-Grillet the world is neither absurd nor meaningful; it simply is. Therefore, the traditional chronological-linear plot, which suggests order and meaning, should be abandoned in favor of a form which uses flashback and disconnection in such a way that no coherent pattern can be reconstructed from them. While Robbe-

Grillet would deny that the world has any preestablished order, he believes that it is the purpose of the novel—with the help of the reader—to bring partial and provisional significations to expression. Robbe-Grillet, then, seems to suggest that the novel can create continuity between man and a limited configuration of meaningful worldly reality, and the novelist-critic strongly insists on the independent substantiality of things. But does he not move in another direction when he insists so strongly on the novel's radically subjective view of the world? The novel does not mirror reality; it constitutes it. And where is the reality that it constitutes? It is not in the world or between man and the world. Rather for Robbe-Grillet the "more" real—which we suspect for him means the "really" real—is found in the mind and imagination.[77] Roland Barthes is not satisfied with a text that has a determinate meaning or even with one that has an indeterminate plurality of meanings. No, the only kind of text that should be written today is one which has an infinite number of entries and which is so open that it can be completed only by the reader and in a different way every time he reads it.[78] As modern apocalyptic has tended toward fully realized apocalyptic in its secularized form, it has not been able to forgo a locus of salvation outside of the world of history; it has rather substituted for God's new transcendent world the interiority of the human mind—while in Mark a renewed history is itself exploding with unexpected possibilities.

If there is in the apocalyptic configuration a tendency toward fully realized apocalyptic, toward the absolutizing of the third element in the configuration (gnosticism in the ancient world, the various ways of criticizing order and structure in modern apocalyptic), what is the motive power behind this tendency?[79] Perhaps it is the comic view vis-à-vis an intolerable world: the world is intolerable, but you can get out. I suggested that in the ancient period the kerygma (death and resurrection is the nucleus of the comic form) could have been the catalyst[80] that turned—or helped to turn—apocalyptic into gnosticism. May it be that for apocalyptic in general the catalytic moving power is the comic sense of life? Gnosticism or fully realized apocalyptic is one way of perceiving man's being picked up, or picking himself up again, after being knocked down.

This poses a problem which I will not attempt to solve or even to deal with in this book. I am trying to show that both Paul and Mark express the comic view, and I have just suggested that the same is true for over-realized apocalyptic novels (and gnostic Gospels). But what is the generic-structural relationship of the latter to the former? This is the problem that I am leaving untouched. The two groups of texts that I have mentioned here— (1) Paul and Mark; (2) gnostic Gospels and novels—are both comic but do not belong to the same genre. This acknowledgment is in line with what I have already suggested, if not asserted, about my purpose. I am not trying to establish *the* comic genre but *a* "nonconventional" comic genre which might be useful for New Testament hermeneutic.

C. A Closer Approach to the Markan Genre

The term *gospel* meant originally good tidings and was characteristically used in the Roman world of the good news emanating from the emperor's birthday or enthronement. The Old Testament (Isa. 52:7) used the verbal form of the word for the good news about Yahweh's reign, but biblical Hebrew had no corresponding noun form.[81] "Gospel" in Mark 1:1 is the *title* of the Evangelist's story about Jesus,[82] and says nothing in itself about gospel as genre, even if the term was not used again as the title of a book until Justin used it in A.D. 150.[83] For Mark gospel is a form which makes Jesus present.[84]

At this point I discuss certain positions on the question of why Mark was written in the hope of arriving at one—at least provisionally—of my own. Some views on the matter express positions that are too broad to account for the particularity of Mark or are not broad enough to be more than partial. At one end of the spectrum are the opinions that the Gospel was written because the original bearers of the tradition were no longer available[85] or was written to persuade nonbelievers and to meet the needs of the church.[86] At the other end of the spectrum is the opinion that Jesus had to be made to appear innocent at his trial.[87] Neill Q. Hamilton argues that Mark expected the resurrected lord to return as the translated Son of Man who would have an earthly career analogous to his first one, except in power and glory (9:1; 13:26; 14:62).

Thus Mark wrote to portray an appropriate first career.[88] But if that were really Mark's purpose, why did he have so much to say about the first career—and in historical-narrative form—and so little to say about the second "glorified" career?

There are other positions on why Mark was written. They answer the question in terms of a theological intention which has both breadth and particularity and which sees this intention and conceptuality as aimed at a definite historical situation. Many believe that Mark was written to correct a false (divine man) Christology[89] by combining it with or moderating it in the light of a suffering Son of Man Christology[90] or combining it with a semi-gnostic kerygmatic motif such as that reflected in Phil. 2:6–11.[91] This christological reflection is typically seen to be motivated and evoked by factors—the false christological belief and the conception of discipleship resulting from it, or vice-versa—which existed in Mark's historical situation. According to Schreiber in particular, Mark was polemicizing against Palestinian Jewish Christianity because the latter had failed to see the crucified one as the exalted one and had also neglected to recognize his presence among the gentile Christians.[92] Mark's Christology as Schreiber defines it might have carried some weight against the first of these deficiencies, but one fails to see its necessary or logical connection with the second.

Kelber also holds that the theology of the Gospel in its redactional form was worked out "in response to current events."[93] However, in his judgment the current event in Mark's situation was an eschatological rather than a christological heresy. Mark's opponents had tied the parousia of Christ to the fall of Jerusalem, and they even believed that the return of Christ was occurring *in them*. But the failure of the parousia to coincide with the fall of Jerusalem had divested the parousia of its hope. Mark wanted to rescue the parousia as a genuine future hope by detaching it from its connection with a historical event.[94] Kelber has a number of helpful things to say about Mark, but I do not believe that he has successfully correlated his statement that the hermeneutical key to Mark is the strong note of fulfillment in 1:14–15 with his further assertion that Mark is an "apocalyptic vision."[95] Marxsen also holds that Mark had an apocalyptic purpose (at least at times; his position is not altogether clear). The whole tenor of the Gospel is colored by the expectation of the imminent parousia. Mark is warning those who are still in Judea to flee to Galilee where Jesus will appear.[96]

The final comprehensive purpose for the writing of Mark to be mentioned is that Mark somehow saw that the word of God could not be adequately expressed in brief kerygmatic formulas or in isolated stories about Jesus or sayings by him. The word needed to take the form of a total historical narrative.[97] Going back to Kähler, we find something of the same thing in mind in the assertion that Mark is a passion narrative with an elaborated introduction. Mark to a large extent was written backward from the passion narrative.[98]

My response to the foregoing is that those who say that Mark wrote in order to combat heresy usually do not explain very precisely, if at all, why Mark's particular kind of narrative was necessary or especially appropriate for countering the particular heresy in mind. There seems rather to be a kind of assumption that Mark did it this way because the materials were available. But there must be a better reason. After all Paul combatted heresy—maybe even a divine man heresy in 2 Corinthians—in letters. The fight against heresy does not require narrative. Those who say that Mark wrote a narrative in order to expand the kerygma or the passion narrative or to give a framework to fragments of the tradition often do not explain why he did this or what it accomplishes.

Robinson and Koester, as we have observed, do offer something concrete when they hold that the form-and-content of the Markan narrative acts to restrain the gnostic tendencies of a sayings source (Q). Marxsen seems to be on to something when he states that Mark consolidated all of his materials into one sermon in order to identify the earthly Jesus (of the past) with the exalted lord (of the present and future).[99] But this insight is vitiated by his denial of much of Mark's narrative or story character (for example, chronology and representation, to be discussed in Chapter IV). Perrin does a better job of accounting for the significance of narrative when he states that Mark involves the reader in a story that began with Jesus and leads into the reader's own time,[100] although I disagree with Perrin's near classification of Mark as apocalypse.

Käsemann, writing about the Synoptics in general rather than about Mark in particular, reminds us that our decisions are always determined by the past. We are always in a kairos which overlaps the moment of decision and which affects what possibilities are open or closed. The Synoptics describe the kairos which began with Jesus and hence the possibilities of those who belong to that kairos.[101] The historicizing narrative asserts the primacy of Christ over the community and affirms the importance of the historical Jesus against an enthusiasm which perhaps thought that it could do without him.[102] If one is going to approach the question of Mark's purpose from a historical-theological standpoint (and that is an important standpoint), one can hardly do better than Käsemann. In the preceding section of this chapter I tried to show with some concrete detail the nature of the kairos opened up by Jesus as Mark understood it. But one does not have to ask why Mark wrote his Gospel in the form in which he wrote it. One can bracket out the presuppositions that usually go with that question and ask rather how Mark happened to be written.

Mark came to be written because the/a kerygma proclaiming, and the faith in, the death and resurrection of Jesus reverberated in the mind of Mark and activated the comic genre whose nucleus is also death and resurrection. (Jesus, kerygma, and believing community are historical phenomena.) The story took the shape it did because the comic genre—a deep, generative structure of the human mind—generated the Gospel of Mark as a performance text, a transformation of itself (see figure 4, Chapter II, and figure 17, Chapter IV, for representations of how the nuclear image death/resurrection unfolds itself in the comic genre). Into this scheme may be placed Ricoeur's observation that symbols tend to expand into larger conceptual worlds or signifying totalities.[103] All of the factors in Mark's historical situation (the divine man heresy, the threat of gnosticism or enthusiasm, Christian prophets claiming to be Christ returned or divine men themselves, the failure of the parousia hope, the fall of Jerusalem, etc., and the texts and traditions reflecting all of these phenomena), all these factors were simply the stuff lying around out of which Mark made the story— the *bricoles* (perhaps the French term will less offend the ears of the New Testament critic-historian than the English "debris").

To suppose that the historical phenomena somehow caused the

text of Mark is to assume that language is an icon, that the text is primarily a reflection of a historical reality outside of itself. This view fails to recognize that both texts and history as meaningful are generated by "grammars" or systems of meaning, linguistic competences which are substructures of a fundamental matrix of possibilities of meaning. It has never been proved that the grammar of history is ontologically or epistemologically prior to the grammar (genre) of texts.[104]

Before pursuing further the question of what the Markan genre is I should like to look briefly at some reasons offered by New Testament scholars for pursuing the question of genre at all. Genre analysis may be made subservient to historical criticism. J. Arthur Baird regards the Synoptics as a mode, or a temporary or artificial genre, rather than as a genre in the full sense. But to the extent that the Gospels are a genre, he wants to use their generic features as a means for pushing back to the purposes and processes in the historical situation which produced the Synoptic genre, and ultimately he wants to arrive at the historical Jesus. He argues, for example, that realism and brilliance of detail are evidence for eyewitness historical authenticity.[105] But such traits could just as well be evidence for poetic vividness or effective fictitious representation of the world. Norman Petersen also considers genre determination to be a means of historical understanding and reconstruction.[106] But he does recognize genre as an independent magnitude and not merely as the end product of an evolutionary process in the tradition.[107] Yet the gestalt character of the finished gospel text is not always kept in view.[108] In recognizing the effect of genre upon the tradition Petersen states that it is not what Jesus did and said that determined the genre but rather how what happened to him was construed.[109] As a substitute for this statement, or as a dialectical addition to it, I would want to say: It was not the construing of what Jesus did and said that determined the genre, but the genre that determined how what he did and said was construed.

Contrary to the title of Baird's article, genre analysis is an aspect of literary criticism, *not* a method of historical criticism. The lines which run from a text to its genre (a linguistic generative matrix) are then extended, not to the text's historical setting, but to *lit-*

térarité—that reservoir of formal literary possibilities. Genre analysis is then hardly a tool for historical reconstruction.

The quest for genre may also be pursued in the effort to discover what the author intended to say.[110] But to discover that an author intended to use a particular genre is as difficult as to discover why he intended to write a particular work. That one can discover such an intention has long been considered a fallacy by "new criticism"[111] and is now so considered by structuralism.[112] The opinion that genre is a way of access to the author's intention might be of some validity if genre is conceived in the broadest possible way: He intended to write a novel; he intended to write a play. But how much does that tell us about the particular work? Even if he intended to write a novel he might have actually written a romance. Or he may have intended to be quite realistic but let his symbols get the best of him. Or he may have started a tragedy which ended up a comedy. E. D. Hirsh, on whom Petersen depends, has some good points to make about the nature of genre. But his argument that an author's intention may be determined on the basis of his genre[113] proceeds largely by ignoring phenomenology's critique of the subject/object dichotomy; that is, the author's intention is seen as a discrete, ascertainable object. It is one thing to argue that the representatives of a genre can usually be counted upon to follow the genre's principles. It is something else to claim that a given author intended to write that particular work in that particular genre.

It is profitable to determine that a work *does* belong to a particular genre or that it departs from the genre which it seems to belong to in certain ways and, therefore, is ambiguous or simply confused. But I think that one cannot discover very much about what an author *intended* to mean on the basis of generic determination, although one may receive considerable light in understanding what a text *does* mean. Genre may be a hermeneutical vantage point.

What then is the Markan genre? Again I will work through several positions in the effort to arrive at one which commends itself to me. It is possible to maintain that there is no such thing as a gospel genre because all of the Gospels are too dissimilar from each other to form a class.[114] This position assumes—probably correctly—that a one-member class is not a helpful category. But in the case of the Gospels do we really have to do with four one-member classes?

One may also hold that gospel is a kind of truncated genre because canonization prevented its development into a *really* multi-membered class. Bultmann, who takes this position, also regards the Gospels as distinctly Christian creations which have no real parallels or models.[115] Likewise Howard Kee argues that the Gospels were without model or precedent and that none of their ingredients suggested the plan for the whole finished work. Mark was for Kee, however, the creator of a new genre.[116]

Still another answer is that Mark (or the Gospels) was a new literary form or the beginning of a unique genre, but certain models are seen to have influenced it. Schweizer takes this position and holds that the Old Testament historical books and Jonah were perhaps the only models.[117] This may be true but is too broad to be of much help in the quest for Mark's genre. Baird also is in this camp and regards Mark as an expanded apothegm.[118] This is not theoretically impossible because a basic narrative unit can become expanded and complicated in all sorts of ways and become a new formative principle. But does the apothegm commend itself as the model for Mark? An apothegm is a form which in the Gospels is composed of a brief narrative introduction and a saying of Jesus which is the central interest and focal point.[119] It is also sometimes held that an apothegm has a third element, an external rounding off which concludes it;[120] but not all of the apothegms in the Gospels manifest the third feature. With regard to Mark the beginning narrative is too extensive to be called a brief introduction; the teaching is too diffused to be the central focus, and the passion narrative is too important to be an external rounding off.

Along with the popularity of the view that Mark was written to counter a divine man Christology goes the popularity of the opinion that Mark has a generic connection with the aretalogy— the story of a divine man. The aretalogy presented the divine birth of its hero, emphasized his miracles and teaching, and related his death and glorification. It was composed to praise the divine man who was supposed to have performed the deeds recounted, and it carried the belief that divine power was present and available in his acts.[121] Petersen does not think that Mark, Matthew, and Luke belong to the same genre, but he suggests that Mark (and apparently John) belongs to a subtype of aretalogy. Yet, Mark rejected the idea of Jesus as a divine man, for his death and resurrection are not just the culminating event in his life but the radical qualification of it.[122] Smith maintains that the Gospels are more similar to aretalogies than to any other known ancient literary type, but he doubts that these collections of miracle stories were similar in literary form to the Gospels and even questions whether the aretalogy had a precise form.[123] Howard Kee also doubts that aretalogies had any common literary pattern and denies that they provided a model for Mark.[124] Finally both Robinson and Koester recognize an aretalogical element in Mark but affirm that it was made subservient to the passion motif.[125] I must conclude that if there was a genre aretalogy, it was very amorphous; and if Mark used one or more such documents as sources he radically moderated them. Thus we must look further for the generic clue to Mark. There is a need for both more breadth and more precision than aretalogy provides.

At this point I should like to consider certain connections which have been made between Mark (or the Gospels) and larger, well-established genres. Robert Scholes[126] names the Synoptic Gospels among "candidates for a truly great Christian novel." This is a provocative suggestion, but it is too briefly made to be of help for my purposes.

Roland Frye suggests that the Gospels belong to the genre dramatic history. This is not the same thing as historical fiction, which simply uses the past as a point of departure for the author's imagination. Dramatic history remains essentially faithful to the historical tradition. But it feels free to make alterations and to select certain events, or to invent them, in order to symbolize the truth of the whole. Thus dramatic history always has inherently a message or vision to convey. Within this category Frye includes the historical plays of Shakespeare and G. B. Shaw and Robert Sherwood's *Abe Lincoln in Illinois*.[127]

Frye's suggestions ring true to me, and they will remain in the back of my mind as I proceed, but I would still like more precision. A dramatic history, a biography or autobiography, the history of a given epoch—a Gospel—may be tragic or comic. This question must be pursued further. Frye's way of putting things also prompts us to consider the interaction of the symbolic and the representational in Mark (Chapter IV) and the relative weight of the referential and the poetic linguistic functions in the Gospel (later in this chapter).

Mark shares with Greek tragedy a number of elements of mood and structure: a single theme, one plot, one issue to be resolved, one climax, and one message There is in both a relentless movement toward an inevitable end. Curtis Beach, who takes this position, acknowledges that the one significant thing which distinguishes Mark from Greek tragedy is the joyful outcome of the Gospel.[128] Yet this recognition does not prompt Beach to take up the category of comedy.

Kenneth Hamilton discusses the relationship between comedy and the Christian faith, and I should like to indicate several of his ideas and then respond to them. Hamilton concedes that comedy may be fairly serious on the moral and social level but denies that it can be religiously serious. This is because comedy is powerless to deal with death. The resurrection-victory of Christianity is on the far side of tragedy while comedy is on this side of it. Thus the Christian faith can be called comic only in a special sense, and tragedy is the last word about death unless faith perceives something beyond the world. The effort to build a fully sustaining comic celebration of life here and now founders on the fact of death.[129]

Hamilton has ignored the generic seed of comedy in a death-and-resurrection ritual and the concomitant fact that all comedy retains a vestige of this in however transformed a representation. Moreover, Hamilton makes a hiatus between tragic death in this world and a hope beyond the world. Doubtless the New Testament has a hope beyond this world, but that is far from all that it has to say on the subject of death and resurrection. Mark paradoxically unites death and resurrection both narratively and didactically, and, as we have seen, Paul existentially appropriates death and resurrection as a posture for daily life (2 Cor. 4:7–12). The New Testament does not allow Hamilton's pulling apart of death and resurrection. It places both death and resurrection, resurrection-through-death, on *this* side of tragedy—and thus casts a new light on death.

We have seen from the discussion of Beach's position that Mark overflows the genre of tragedy, while for Hamilton comedy is not a sufficiently serious category for grasping the Christian faith— and by implication—the Gospel of Mark.

But what I was trying to suggest in the preceding paragraph is that Hamilton has missed something important which is ingredient in comedy. If Mark is both comic and serious, as I shall argue, then what we need is the genre-category tragicomedy. My thesis for the rest of this chapter and the guiding principle for the next is: Mark as one of the transformations or performance texts generated by the particular genre which I am trying to construct is a tragicomedy.

Tragedy and comedy both arose from essentially the same kind of death and resurrection ritual, and the two genres separated by virtue of whether the emphasis was placed on conflict and death or on resurrection and marriage.[130] We have observed that comedy and tragedy can deal with the same situations, but from different perspectives and with different emphases. The central element in both is conflict.[131]

Prior to the eighteenth century tragicomedy meant a work which mixed various tragic and comic elements in succession. But since that date it has meant a work which fused the two so that both kept their identity and were strengthened while each was made identical with the other. A given situation is seen *simultaneously* as both tragic and comic.[132] Mark might be thought of as tragicomedy in the old sense: death is *followed by* resurrection. But in a number of ways Mark is a "modern" tragicomedy. There is simultaneity of the tragic and comic because the new which finally issues in resurrection is there from the beginning: the time is fulfilled. And the old world, the opposition which penultimately kills Jesus, is also there from the outset. As we shall see there are many sequences in which there is conflict, and Jesus is threatened but victorious. The new Christian community is sustaining but persecuted. Jesus and the Jewish officials maintain simultaneously two opposng points of view on the same actions and ideas (see Chapter IV).

Modern tragicomedy has renounced the metaphysical certainties on which both classical tragedy and comedy rested. But it has also renounced the renunciation of metaphysical *concerns* which has characterized much drama since the nineteenth century. What cannot be unequivocally accepted is not so much denied as questioned. Thus tragicomedy confronts us with uncertainty and skepticism rather than with assertive nihilism.[133] From this standpont Mark is more "modern" than the other Gospels. There is a certain uncertainty about who Jesus is. There are no birth stories or resurrection appearances to prove his status. Mark vividly portrays Jesus' humanity and has Jesus question why he should be called good. Throughout the book Jesus' identity is a problem—an uncertainty —for all who confront him.[134] Yet for the Evangelist himself Jesus is the Son of God. The relationship between these two themes will be discussed in the next chapter.

Karl Guthke shows that tragicomedy achieves its special generic quality and effect by using certain structural patterns, seven of which he lists. He states that any given tragicomedy will usually display two or more of these patterns, and I believe that Mark exhibits four of them.

(1) The work may contrast a character who is fit for tragedy with a world that belongs to comedy.[135] In Mark Jesus' purpose and fate clearly qualify him for tragedy, and he distinctly stands out from the crowd, but his associations and some of his actions belong to the comic. He sits and walks. He chooses fishermen and tax collectors for companions and eats with the riffraff.

(2) The illusionary world of the protagonist is contrasted with the real world which is known to the audience or to other characters. But the protagonist is deceived—by himself or by others— and this deception is what causes the discrepancy between the two worlds. He does not know that his world is unreal.[136] Mark presents a reverse transformation of this pattern. It is Jesus' opponents —of all sorts—who are finally shown to have been deceived about the realities.

(3) The irony in the course of events victimizes the protagonist and brings him to the stature of a tragic hero.[137] The opposition to Jesus culminating in his death ironically brings him to victory while his opponents' apparent victory causes their defeat.

(4) There is a conflict within a person such as between intention and fulfillment, self-image and reality, or appearance and reality.[138] Jesus claims the reality of religious authority, but denies the appear-

ance of it. He acts contrary to established piety, refuses to prove
(8:11–13) or indicate the source of his authority (11:28–33),
and takes at best an ambivalent attitude toward the primary title
of authority (8:29–33). The conflict is between the hidden reality
and the visible appearance. Peter (8:29–33) tempts him to re-
nounce the reality in favor of the appearance.

Mark does not really exploit the comic side of these patterns.
He lets it remain implicit. Mark is primarily tragicomedy because
of the global and detailed presence of the death and *resurrection*
or *life*-through-death motif.

The final thing that I want to do in this chapter is to raise
the question of the relative prominence in Mark of the six primary
speech functions mentioned in Chapter I.

(1) One would not expect the phatic function to be very prominent, and it is not, but it is there. There are occasional reminders
that the channel is open: "Truly, I say to you"; "he who has ears
to hear, let him hear."

(2) The expressive function, that which manifests the inwardness of the narrator, is all but absent. Starobinski in fact asserts that every expressive reference to the author has been
excluded from the Gospel of Mark.[139] We shall see, however, in
Chapter IV that if every expression of the author's *inwardness*
has been removed, that is not the same thing as obliterating every
aspect of his subjectivity.

(3) The conative function is rather prominent. Since the author's own voice is relatively silent, the narrative itself speaks
strongly to the reader. Therefore, the many incidents in which
Jesus calls on men to believe or to follow him or to understand
are also calls to the reader, the recipient of the text.

(4) There is a sense in which Mark is metalinguistic. It is
a commentary upon or interpretation of another text—the/a
kerygma.[140] It is "discourse upon discourse." Mark is one performance text, one transformation, which shows how the image or
nuclear narrative—Jesus was killed and arose from the dead—is
channeled and expanded by the structure of the/a comic genre.
But Mark is not metalinguistic in the usual sense. The metalinguistic
"text upon a text" is usually discursive and analytical. It is ordinar-

ily thought of as exegetical theology done on a biblical passage or literary criticism done on a literary work. But Mark, while it has its didactic aspects, is the anomaly of a metalinguistic narrative.

(5) The matter becomes a bit more complicated when we come to the referential function because narrative elements may have a number of different kinds of referents and may refer in different ways.[141] The same element in fact may have more than one referent or may refer in more than one way.

There may be reference to actual events in the life of the historical Jesus or actual phenomena in Mark's historical situation. Or there may be reference to ideas or motifs in the Old Testament and/or Judaism. We must add to the referential function the fictitious *representation* of the "real" world in such a way that the reader believes that the event or events could have really happened.[142] That Jesus' disciples did not fast (2:18–19a) is probably an actuality of Jesus' ministry, but Jesus' statement that later they would fast (2:20) is undoubtedly a reference to a historical circumstance in the life of Mark's church or some other. Jesus' entry into Jerusalem may refer more or less accurately to something that Jesus really did but it also refers to the motif of the meek king in Zech. 9:9. The story of the last supper probably refers to an unrecoverable event in Jesus' history, and it also refers to the Old Testament motifs of covenant and sacrifice and to current cult practice in Mark's church and/or other churches. That Jesus ate with the outcasts from pious Jewish society and interpreted this theologically would seem to be historically true. Such a mode of interpreted action does not express the characteristically Christian kerygma of the death and resurrection of Jesus or make use of christological titles, and it also reflects a Jewish milieu, but with a difference. Thus this kind of action passes the test of dissimilarity and may be considered a historical reference. But the *particular* story in Mark 2:15–17 may be fictitious representation. And I would submit that it will almost always be impossible, if not always, to distinguish unequivocally between historical reference and fictitious representation in Mark. They are too intertwined.

(6) The Gospel of Mark also strongly exercises the poetic function: it focuses on itself. It has a unified, cohesive, causally connected plot which centers on one unifying protagonist; and it has

a unifying theme. The text is sufficiently organic and centripetally organized to keep attention on itself.[143]

But there is one more thing to be said here about Mark as narrative art. Because it has a certain kind of plot, identifiable character types, an authorial point of view, and other structural features which will be considered in the next chapter, it *refers* in a sense to literary discourse itself or *littérarité*—that indeterminate reservoir of formal possibilities which comprises the linguistic competence of the author and from which the work sprang. Thus even here there is reference. From this angle of vision the work does not refer to something heterogeneous—historical, theological, sociological, or psychological phenomena—but to something homogeneous—literary discourse. Yet it still refers. Thus our discussion of the poetic function has brought us back around to the referential. It should also be pointed out that representation may both be referential *and* contribute to the centripetal tying together of the plot. So which is primary in Mark, the referential or the poetic? Who would give a dogmatic answer? Perhaps it is not so important to answer this question globally as it is to clarify how the language of the text does function.

NOTES TO CHAPTER III

1. C. Chabrol, "Problèmes de la sémiotique narrative des récits bibliques," *Langages* 6, no. 22 (June, 1971): 5–7; see also Edmund Leach, "The Legitimacy of Solomon: Some Structural Aspects of Old Testament History," *European Journal of Sociology* 7, no. 1 (1966): 65–66.

2. Roland M. Frye, "A Literary Perspective for the Criticism of the Gospels," *Jesus and Man's Hope,* II (Pittsburgh: Pittsburgh Theological Seminary, 1971), pp. 194–195, 212–213, 220.

3. Ibid., p. 220.

4. See Leach, "The Legitmacy of Solomon," pp. 65–66, 99; Jean Starobinski, "The Struggle with Legion: A Literary Analysis of Mark 5:1–20," trans. D. Via, *New Literary History* 4, no. 2 (Winter, 1973): 333. Starobinski is the eminent Geneva critic who combines structuralism with "criticism of consciousness."

5. See, for example, Willi Marxsen, *Mark the Evangelist*, trans. J. Boyce, D. Juel, W. Poehlmann, R. Harrisville (Nashville: Abingdon Press, 1969), pp. 28–29; Johannes Schreiber, "Die Christologie des Markusevangeliums," *Zeitschrift für Theologie und Kirche* 58, heft 2 (August, 1961): 154–155; Leander E. Keck, "Mark 3:7–12 and Mark's Christology," *Journal of Biblical Literature* 84, part 4 (December, 1965): 341, 347–348; Morton Smith, "Prolegomena to a Discussion of Aretalogies, Divine Men, the Gospels, and Jesus," *Journal of Biblical Literature* 90, part 2 (June, 1971): 197; Norman Perrin, "The Creative Use of the Son of Man Traditions by Mark," in *A Modern Pilgrimage in New Testament Christology* (Philadelphia: Fortress Press, 1974), chap. VI; Paul J. Achtemeier, "Toward the Isolation of Pre-Markan Miracle Catenae," *Journal of Biblical Literature* 89, part 3 (September, 1970): 273–274, 290–291; Paul J. Achtemeier, "The Origin and Function of the Pre-Markan Miracle Catenae," *Journal of Biblical Literature* 91, no. 2 (June, 1972): 199, 218; James M. Robinson, "On the Gattung of Mark (and John)," *Jesus and Man's Hope,* I, pp. 101, 106; Philipp Vielhauer, "Erwägungen zur Christologie des Markusevangeliums," *Zeit und Geschichte*, ed. E. Dinkler (Tübingen: J. C. B. Mohr, 1964), pp. 156–157; Ernest Best wants to identity peculiarly Markan elements, but he does also conclude that Mark must have largely chosen what he agreed with. However, Best does not go into the question of Mark as a new gestalt: see *The Temptation and the Passion* (Cambridge: Cambridge University Press, 1965), pp. ix, x, 103–104. Curtis Beach (*The Gospel of Mark* [New York: Harper & Row, 1959], pp. 16, 28–33, 37, 40. 52–53, 121) sometimes speaks of Mark as the product of sources, as an additive aggregation, but at other times he recognizes Mark as a new, creative, unity. He has not, however, thoroughly investigated the relationship of the units to the form or penetrated Mark's way of arranging the units. Antonio Gaboury uses the term *structure* in his work, but he, too, wants to maintain the distinction between tradition and redaction, and he questions whether the Evangelists were real authors with unified points of view. His real interest seems to be the source analysis of the Gospels, which he sees as the end product of a processing of tradition; see his "Christological Implications Resulting from a Study of the Structure of the Synoptic Gospels," *Proceedings: Society of Biblical Literature* I

(Society of Biblical Literature, 1972), pp. 99–101, 103–116. James M. Robinson ("The Problem of History in Mark, Reconsidered," *Union Seminary Quarterly Review* 20 [1965]: 133) more or less apologizes for not having done real redactional critical work, for not having kept redaction and tradition distinguished, in his earlier work on Mark *(The Problem of History in Mark)*. It would have been better if he had not apologized but had rather conceptualized and thematized a methodology for keeping tradition and redaction together so that Mark could be seen as a literary whole.

6. Howard C. Kee, *Jesus in History* (New York: Harcourt, Brace, and World, 1970), p. 104; Perrin, "The Christology of Mark: A Study in Methodology," in *A Modern Pilgrimage,* chap. VIII; Robinson, "On the Gattung of Mark (and John)," pp. 104, 107.

7. Keck, "Mark 3:7–12," p. 358.

8. Frye, "Literary Perspective," p. 214.

9. Georg Strecker, "The Passion and Resurrection Predictions in Mark's Gospel," *Interpretation* 22 (October, 1968): 440.

10. Ibid.

11. H. E. Tödt, *The Son of Man in the Synoptic Tradition,* trans. D. Barton (Philadelphia: Westminster Press, 1965), pp. 206–211.

12. See A. J. Greimas, *Sémantique Structurale* (Paris: Librairie Larousse, 1966), p. 195.

13. Roland Barthes, "Introduction à l'analyse structurale des récits," *Communications* 8 (1966): 6–10; see Starobinski, "The Struggle with Legion," pp. 338–339.

14. Theodore J. Weeden, *Mark—Traditions in Conflict* (Philadelphia: Fortress Press, 1971), pp. 2–3, 103, 164.

15. Ibid., pp. 162–163.

16. Roland Barthes, *Critical Essays,* trans. R. Howard (Evanston: Northwestern University Press, 1972), pp. 250–251.

17. Weeden, *Mark,* pp. 11–14.

18. Ibid., pp. 26–27, 32–34, 38, 54–59.

19. Ibid., p. 56. On p. 154 Weeden moderates this position somewhat.

20. Ibid., pp. 44, 50, 117.

21. Keck, "Mark 3:7–12," pp. 349, 351.

22. Erhardt Güttgemanns, *Offene Fragen zur Formgeschichte des Evangeliums* (München: Christian Kaiser Verlag, 1970), pp. 19, 32–33, 228–229, 259.

23. Ibid., pp. 75–76.

24. Ibid., pp. 70, 78–79, 87–88, 148, 152–153. Form criticism has usually assumed that the oral tradition must have behaved—expressed the same kind of tendencies—very much as the written tradition did. See Rudolf Bultmann, *The History of the Synoptic Tradition,* trans. J. Marsh (New York: Harper & Row, 1963), p. 6; this is also the working hypothesis in E. P. Sanders, *The Tendencies of the Synoptic Tradition* (Cambridge: Cambridge University Press, 1969; Society for New Testament Studies Monograph Series, no 9), pp. 8–9, 280. The work of Parry on oral traditions, however, has shown that oral literature is highly "formulaic": groups of words are regularly employed under the same metrical conditions to express a given essential idea. The language is controlled by a limited number of patterns selected from the total language of the culture. Written literature

is not formulaic. Therefore, it may be concluded that written texts do not have a high degree of relevance for the study of oral tradition. See Robert Scholes and Robert Kellogg, *The Nature of Narrative* (London, Oxford, and New York: Oxford University Press, 1971; copyright, 1966), pp. 20, 31, 40, 50. The only way to discover what portions of the Synoptic Gospels are "close" to the oral tradition is to go through all of the Synoptic material very carefully, identifying those sections which are highly formulaic.

25. Güttgemanns, *Offene Fragen*, pp. 87, 90, 91, 139, 185–187.

26. Ibid., pp. 224, 228.

27. Ibid., pp. 195, 197, 207, 210, 223.

28. Ibid., pp. 237–238.

29. Ibid., pp. 240–243, 246, 248–250.

30. See Kurt Müller-Vollmer, *Towards a Phenomenological Theory of Literature* (The Hague: Mouton and Co., 1963), pp. 106–107.

31. Maurice Merleau-Ponty, *The Visible and the Invisible*, trans. A. Lingis (Evanston: Northwestern University Press, 1968), pp. 131, 133–139.

32. Paul Ricoeur, *De l'interprétation* (Paris: Editions du Seuil, 1965), pp. 47–48.

33. Güttgemanns, *Offene*, p. 223.

34. Ibid., pp. 198, 224–226.

35. See Sarah N. Lawall, *Critics of Consciousness* (Cambridge: Harvard University Press, 1968), pp. 139, 266–267.

36. Tzvetan Todorov, "Les catégories du récit littéraire," *Communications* 8 (1966): 146–147.

37. In dependence on Merleau-Ponty this point is made in Eugene F. Kaelin, *An Existentialist Aesthetic* (Madison: University of Wisconsin Press, 1962), p. 329.

38. E. D. Hirsch, *Validity in Interpretation* (New Haven: Yale University Press, 1967), pp. 8, 72–74, 78, 89–90, 102–103; Helmut Koester, "The Origin and Nature of Diversification in the History of Early Christianity," *Harvard Theological Review* 58 (1965): 300; Norman R. Petersen, Jr., "So-Called Gnostic Type Gospels and the Question of the Genre 'Gospel' " (unpublished paper, 1970), pp. 14, 16, 20, 29, 49. I do not agree with all of the details expressed in these references but only with the broad point of the connection between genre and meaning. D. E. Nineham (*The Gospel of St. Mark* [Baltimore: Penguin Books, 1967; Pelican Gospel Commentaries], p. 37) seems to see no important or inherent connection between narrative form and theological meaning.

39. Perrin, "Christology," chap. VIII.

40. Norman Perrin, "Historical Criticism, Literary Criticism, and Hermeneutics: The Interpretation of the Parables of Jesus and the Gospel of Mark Today," *The Journal of Religion* 52, no. 4 (October, 1972): 365–366, 372.

41. Werner Kelber, "The History of the Kingdom in Mark—Aspects of Markan Eschatology," *Proceedings: Society of Biblical Literature* I (Society of Biblical Literature, 1972), p. 86.

42. Kee, *Jesus*, pp. 129–130, 137–140; Weeden, *Mark*, pp. 85, 88, 89–92, 159; Nineham, *Gospel of St. Mark*, pp. 355, 359. Marxsen (*Mark*, pp. 85, 92, 112–113, 188–189) finally hedges on the question of whether Mark is really apocalyptic.

43. Perrin, "Historical Criticism," pp. 369, 372, 373.
44. See Scholes and Kellogg, *Narrative*, pp. 82–91; Barthes, "Introduction," pp. 4–6.
45. Perrin, "Son of Man," chap. VI; "Christology," chap. VIII.
46. See Philipp Vielhauer, "Apocalyptic," pp. 583–587; "Apocalyptic in Early Christianity: Introduction," *New Testament Apocrypha* II, ed. Hennecke, Schneemelcher, Wilson, trans. Best, et al. (Philadelphia: Westminster Press, 1964), p. 620; D. S. Russell, *The Method and Message of Jewish Apocalyptic* (Philadelphia: Westminster Press, 1964), pp. 118–130, 158.
47. See Russell, *Jewish Apocalyptic,* pp. 105–106, 108, 125, 185, 220–284; Vielhauer, "Apocalyptic," pp. 588–593; S. Mowinckel, *He That Cometh,* trans. G. W. Anderson (New York and Nashville: Abingdon Press, 1954; first published 1951), pp. 261, 263–264, 268, 274–275; Christopher R. North, *The Old Testament Interpretation of History* (London: Epworth Press, 1953), pp. 136–137; H. H. Rowley, *The Relevance of Apocalyptic* (New York: Association Press, 1963; rev. ed.), pp. 166–168, 173, 178–179, 183; Otto Plöger, *Theocracy and Eschatology,* trans. S. Rudman (Richmond: John Knox Press, 1968), pp. 17, 28–29; Gerhard von Rad, *Old Testament Theology* II, trans. D. M. G. Stalker (New York: Harper & Row, 1965), pp. 302–305; William G. Doty, "Identifying Eschatological Language," *Continuum* 7 (1970): 552; Hans Dieter Betz, "The Concept of Apocalyptic in the Theology of the Pannenberg Group," *Journal for Theology and the Church* 6: *Apocalypticism*, ed. R. Funk, trans. J. Leitch (New York: Herder & Herder, 1969): 201–202; David Noel Freedman, "The Flowering of Apocalyptic," *Journal for Theology and the Church* 6 (1969): 169–170.
48. Rowley, *Apocalyptic*, pp. 168–170; Russell, *Jewish Apocalyptic*, pp. 105–106, 205, 220, 224.
49. Klaus Koch, *The Rediscovery of Apocalyptic*, trans. M. Kohl (London: SCM Press, 1972; Studies in Biblical Theology, Second Series, 22), pp. 14, 41–42, 44, 91, 102–103, 131.
50. Mowinckel, *He That Cometh*, p. 264; Betz, "Apocalyptic in the Pannenberg Group," pp. 201–202; von Rad, *Old Testament Theology*, pp. 302–305; Vielhauer, "Apocalyptic," p. 592.
51. Koch, *Apocalyptic*, pp. 29–31.
52. Vielhauer ("Christologie," pp. 168–169) has argued this position, and the essential correctness of it will be further defended in Chapter IV.
53. See James M. Robinson, *The Problem of History in Mark* (London: SCM Press, 1957; Studies in Biblical Theology, no 21), p. 55; Kelber, "The History of the Kingdom in Mark," p. 75; Eduard Schweizer, "Mark's Contribution to the Quest of the Historical Jesus," *New Testament Studies* 10 (1963–64): 430.
54. See Kelber, "The History of the Kingdom in Mark," p. 64; also Robinson, *Mark*, p. 52.
55. See Kelber, "The History of the Kingdom in Mark," p. 70; Best, *Temptation*, pp. 65–67.
56. Robinson, *Mark*, pp. 28, 34, 50; Starobinski, "The Struggle with Legion," pp. 338–339, 346–347, 352.
57. See William A. Beardslee, "The Motif of Fulfillment in the Eschatology of the Early Church," *Transitions in Biblical Scholarship*, ed. J. C. Rylaarsdam

(Chicago and London: University of Chicago Press, 1968), p. 183.

58. See Robinson, *Mark,* pp. 60–61; Weeden, *Mark,* pp. 89–90; Kelber believes that Mark's theological opponents had identified the parousia with the fall of Jerusalem; thus when Jerusalem fell, but the parousia did not occur, hope was shattered. Mark attempted to renew hope by detaching the parousia from a particular historical event and maintaining its true imminent futurity and also by anchoring the kingdom in Jesus' historical ministry (see "The History of the Kingdom in Mark," pp. 80–85). Kelber does not explain how the kingdom which occurred in Galilee can be present for Mark's church.

59. Vielhauer, "Apocalyptic in Early Christianity," pp. 608–609; Robert W. Funk, "Apocalyptic as an Historical and Theological Problem in Current New Testament Scholarship," *Journal for Theology and the Church* 6: 182–183.

60. T. A. Burkill (*Mysterious Revelation: An Examination of the Philosophy of St. Mark's Gospel* [Ithaca: Cornell University Press, 1963], pp. 176–179) has argued that Mark ordinarily separates Jesus' present and future as the time of suffering and the time of glory but that sometimes this bipolarity is transcended in that occasionally the present is also seen as the time of glory. Future and present are, so to speak, fused. Burkill seems to see this as a kind of vacillation or lack of control on Mark's part, but it may be a necessary dialectic between temporality as chronology and temporality as qualification of existence.

61. See Eduard Schweizer, *The Good News According to Mark,* trans. D. Madvig (Richmond: John Knox Press, 1970), pp. 102–103; Nineham, *Gospel of St. Mark,* pp. 141–142.

62. The parable chapter calls for more discussion later.

63. The gnostic revelation could also take the form of longer discourses or dialogues, as in the Gospel of Philip and the Apocryphon of John. On this see James M. Robinson, "*LOGOI SOPHON.* On the Gattung of Q." *Trajectories through Early Christianity* (Philadelphia: Fortress Press, 1971), chap. 3; Helmut Koester, "One Jesus and Four Primitive Gospels," *Trajectories through Early Christianity* (Philadelphia: Fortress Press, 1971), pp. 167–168; W. Schneemelcher, "Introduction: Gospel," *New Testament Apocrypha* I, ed. Hennecke, Schneemelcher, Wilson, trans. Higgins, Wilson, et al. (Philadelphia: Westminster Press, 1963), p. 82.

64. Robinson, "Q," chap. 3; Koester, "Origin," pp. 298–302; "One Jesus," p. 179.

65. Koester, "One Jesus," p. 196. Koester implies in this article that the canonical Gospels, sayings collections, aretalogies, and apocalypses are different genres. It, therefore, confuses the issue when he also calls all of these "gospels."

66. See Pheme Perkins, "Apocalyptic Schematization in the Apocalypse of Adam and the Gospel of the Egyptians," *Proceedings: Society of Biblical Literature II* (Society of Biblical Literature, 1972), pp. 591–592; Charles W. Hedrick, "The Apocalypse of Adam: A Literary and Source Analysis," *Proceedings: Society of Biblical Literature* II (Society of Biblical Literature, 1972), p. 590.

67. R. M. Grant, *Gnosticism and Early Christianity* (New York: Harper &

Row, 1966; rev. ed.), pp. 34–37; for the internalizing of apocalyptic as a source of gnosticism see also David Noel Freedman, "The Flowering of Apocalyptic," p. 174.

68. Ernst Käsemann, "On the Subject of Primitive Christian Apocalyptic," *New Testament Questions Today*, trans. J. Montague (Philadelphia: Fortress Press, 1969), pp. 125–127, 129, 130, 131–132, 134–137.

69. See Robinson, "Q," chap. 3; Koester, "Origin," pp. 298, 301; "One Jesus," p. 198.

70. Robinson, "Gattung," pp. 119–126.

71. See Hedrick, "The Apocalypse of Adam," pp. 583–585.

72. Jürgen Moltmann, *Theology of Hope*, trans. J. Leitch (New York: Harper & Row, 1967), pp. 16, 18, 21, 69, 100, 102, 136–137.

73. See R. W. B. Lewis, "Days of Wrath and Laughter," *Trials of the Word* (New Haven and London: Yale University Press, 1965), pp. 220–227.

74. Ibid., pp. 200–202.

75. Nathan A. Scott, Jr., " 'New Heav'ns, New Earth'—the Landscape of Contemporary Apocalypse," *The Journal of Religion* 53, no. 1 (January, 1973): 10–16, 20, 24.

76. See Earl Rovit, "On the Contemporary Apocalyptic Imagination," *The American Scholar* 37 (Summer, 1968): 464–466.

77. Alain Robbe-Grillet, *For a New Novel*, trans. R. Howard (New York: Grove Press, 1965), pp. 9, 12, 19, 21, 32–33, 73, 138, 141, 144, 151–154, 156, 161–162.

78. Roland Barthes, *S/Z* (Paris: Editions du Seuil, 1970), pp. 10–12, 14, 19, 22, 23.

79. Thomas Altizer states that New Testament apocalyptic and modern apocalyptic have in common the fact that they are "fully realized" apocalyptic, and he seems to imply that this is true of all apocalyptic texts ("The Dialectic of Ancient and Modern Apocalypticism," *Journal of the American Academy of Religion* 39, no. 3 [September, 1971]: 312, 318). But we have seen that certainly not all New Testament apocalyptic is fully realized, nor is all modern apocalyptic. See Nils A. Dahl, "Paul and the Church at Corinth According to 1 Corinthians 1:10–4:21," *Christian History and Interpretation*, ed. Farmer, Moule, and Niebuhr, p. 332; J. L. Martyn, "Epistemology at the Turn of the Ages: 2 Cor. 5:16," in *Christian History and Interpretation*, ed. Farmer, Moule, and Niebuhr, pp. 284–286.

Susan Sontag serves the spirit of fully realized apocalyptic when she condemns interpretation as usually practiced as "the revenge of the intellect upon art." What she opposes is the effort to relate art (including literature) to an ordered world of meaning. What she would allow in place of interpretation is a description of the immediate, sensuous surfaces of art *(Against Interpretation* [New York: Dell, Delta Book, 1966], pp. 7–10, 12–13). We can sympathize with her belief that we need to feel more without accepting the implication that that requires understanding less.

80. This would be supported by the fact that some of Paul's statements (such as 2 Cor. 5:16–17; 6:2), if viewed apart from his futuristic eschatalogy, could be considered over-realized (see James M. Robinson, "Kerygma and History in the New Testament," *The Bible in Modern Scholarship*, ed. J. P. Hyatt [Nashville: Abingdon Press, 1965], pp. 142–143). Also the Corinthian

enthusiasts themselves, as well as the slightly gnosticizing authors of Colossians and Ephesians, may have owed something to Paul's realized eschatology.

81. See Schweizer, *Mark*, p. 30; Kee, *Jesus*, pp. 116–118; Schneemelcher, "Introduction," pp. 71–72.

82. Marxsen, *Mark*, p. 117.

83. See Schweizer, *Mark*, p. 30; Schneemelcher, "Introduction," p. 75.

84. See Marxsen, *Mark*, pp. 128–129; Schneemelcher ("Introduction," p. 74), on the other hand, believes that Mark sees his Gospel as an illustration of the message of salvation in Christ rather than as identical with it.

85. Schneemelcher, "Introduction," p. 75.

86. Ninehem, *Gospel of St. Mark*, pp. 19–20, 29.

87. Ibid., p. 366.

88. Neill Q. Hamilton, "Resurrection Tradition and the Composition of Mark," *Journal of Biblical Literature* 84, no. 4 (December, 1965): 420–421.

89. See note 45 for Perrin; see also Keck, "Mark 3:7–12," p. 357; Robinson, "Gattung," pp. 105–106; Schreiber, "Christologie," pp. 156, 158, 163; Petersen; "So-Called Gnostic Type Gospels," pp. 62–63; Weeden, *Mark*, pp. 25–26, 56, 117, 121; Achtemeier, "Origin and Function," pp. 209, 210.

90. Perrin, "Son of Man," chap. VI; Weeden, *Mark*, p. 155; Robinson, "Gattung," pp. 105–106.

91. Schreiber, "Christologic," pp. 156, 158, 163.

92. Ibid., pp. 176–179.

93. Kelber, "The History of the Kingdom in Mark," pp. 63, 89.

94. Ibid., pp. 84, 80–82.

95. Ibid., pp. 65, 86.

96. Marxsen, *Mark*, pp. 85, 133–134, 181–183, 205.

97. See Schweizer, *Mark*, p. 24; "Mark's," pp. 421–422; Kee, *Jesus*, pp. 119, 123, 128.

98. See Marxsen, *Mark*, pp. 30–31.

99. Ibid., p. 94.

100. Perrin, "Historical Criticism," p. 372.

101. Ernst Käsemann, "The Problem of the Historical Jesus," *Essays on New Testament Themes*, trans. W. J. Montague (London: SCM Press, 1964), p. 33.

102. Käsemann, "Blind Alleys in the 'Jesus of History' Controversy," *New Testament Questions of Today*, trans. W. J. Montague (Philadelphia: Fortress Press, 1969), pp. 40–41, 63.

103. Ricoeur, *L'interprétation*, pp. 47–48.

104. See my discussion of Güttgemanns in Chapter I and especially his "'Text' und 'Geschichte' als Grundkategorien der Generativen Poetik," *Linguistica Biblica* 11/12 (January, 1972): pp. 3–5, 9, 12; "Qu'est-ce que la Poétique Générative?" *Linguistica Biblica* 19 (September, 1972): 4.

105. J. Arthur Baird, "Genre Analysis as a Method of Historical Criticism," *Proceedings: Society of Biblical Literature* II (Society of Biblical Literature, 1972), pp. 385, 387, 390, 400, 408.

106. Petersen, "So-Called Gnostic Type Gospels," pp. 4–5.

107. Ibid., pp. 11–14, 31–33, 40, 45–47, 54–55.

108. Ibid., pp. 64–65.

109. Ibid., p. 55.

110. Ibid., pp. 14, 16, 20, 49.

111. For example William K. Wimsatt and Monroe C. Beardsley, *The Verbal Icon* (Lexington: University of Kentucky Press, 1954), pp. 3–4, 10.

112. See François Bovon, "Le structuralisme français et l'exégèse biblique," *Analyse Structurale et Exégèse Biblique* (Neuchâtel: Delachaux et Niestlé, 1971), p. 20.

113. Hirsch, *Validity in Interpretation*, pp. 72–74, 89–90, 113.

114. Marxsen, *Mark*, pp. 105, 212.

115. Rudolf Bultmann, *Synoptic Tradition*, pp. 373–374. Schneemelcher ("Introduction," pp. 76–77) also contends that the Gospels cannot be closely connected with any pre-Christian or non-Christian literature, and he assumes the typical tradition-history view that a completed Gospel is simply the last stage of an evolutionary process.

116. Kee, *Jesus*, pp. 122–123, 126–127.

117. Schweizer, *Mark*, pp. 23–24.

118. Baird, "Genre Analysis," pp. 399, 411.

119. Bultmann, *Synoptic Tradition*, p. 11; Vincent Taylor, *The Formation of the Gospel Tradition* (London: Macmillan, 1949; 2d ed.), pp. 30, 63, 65; Martin Dibelius, *From Tradition to Gospel*, trans. B. L. Woolf (New York: Charles Scribner's Sons, n.d.; from rev. 2d ed.), pp. 48–49, 56.

120. Dibelius, *Tradition*, p. 44.

121. See M. Smith, "Prolegomena," pp. 176, 179; Koester, "One Jesus," pp. 187–188; Achtemeier, "Origin and Function," pp. 203–204, 209; Petersen, "So-Called Gnostic Type Gospels," pp. 64–65; Clyde W. Votaw, *The Gospels and Contemporary Biographies in the Greco-Roman World* (Philadelphia: Fortress Press, 1970; Facet Books, Biblical Series—27, ed. J. Reumann), pp. vi, 5, 11, 21, 62.

122. Petersen, "So-Called Gnostic Type Gospels," pp. 26–29, 65–66.

123. Smith, "Prolegomena," pp. 179, 196.

124. Kee, *Jesus*, pp. 122, 134.

125. Robinson, "Gattung," pp. 105–106; Koester, "One Jesus," p. 198.

126. Robert Scholes, "The Illiberal Imagination" (unpublished paper, Modern Language Association, New York, 1972), forthcoming in *New Literary History*, pp. 4–5.

127. Frye, "Literary Perspective," pp. 207–211, 219.

128. Beach, *Mark*, pp. 48–50.

129. Kenneth Hamilton, "Comedy in a Theological Perspective," *Religion in Life* 41 (Summer, 1972): 330–332.

130. Francis M. Cornford, *The Origin of Attic Comedy* (Cambridge: Cambridge University Press, 1934), pp. 190, 212.

131. Karl S. Guthke, *Modern Tragicomedy* (New York: Random House, 1966), pp. 51–52.

132. Ibid., pp. 6–12, 18, 43, 45.

133. Ibid., pp. 97, 100, 115, 117, 118, 170.

134. See Wayne Rollins, *The Gospels, Portraits of Christ* (Philadelphia: Westminster Press, 1963), pp. 24–49.

135. Guthke, *Modern Tragicomedy*, p. 78.

136. Ibid., p. 81.

137. Ibid., pp. 82–83.

138. Ibid., pp. 84–85.

139. Starobinski, *"The Struggle with Legion,"* p. 334.

140. See Koester, "One Jesus," pp. 162–163.

141. Tzvetan, Todorov ("Poétique," *Qu'est-ce que le structuralisme?* ed. François Wahl [Paris: Editions du Seuil, 1968], p. 108) states that reference is the capacity of a sign to refer to or evoke something other than itself.

142. See Scholes and Kellogg, *Narrative*, pp. 84–86.

143. See Eliseo Vivas, *The Artistic Transaction* (Columbus: Ohio State University Press, 1963), pp. 12, 17, 19–32, 38, 49–51, 57, 61, 63, 157–159.

A Structural Analysis
of the Markan Narrative

My analysis of the Gospel of Mark will be partial and illustrative but hopefully suggestive. A full structural analysis would be virtually endless. It would relate the text to the corpus (genre) to which it belongs and break it down into minimal components until every element had been accounted for and the totality exhausted.[1] Moreover, even a "classical" text like Mark is susceptible to a number of different readings, depending on what signified one approaches the text with.[2] Thus one can see that a complete structural analysis of Mark would require a very long book, or maybe several.

The first, and longer, part of this chapter (A) will deal with Mark internally, and the second part (B) will deal with Mark's generic relationship, although an absolute separation is not possible.

A. Internal Analysis

The meaning of a narrative does not depend solely on the relationship among elements within one level—such as the pattern or kind of connections holding together the actions in the plot. Rather a narrative has several levels, and meaning also depends on the relationships among these levels. It is vertical as well as horizontal; therefore, the structure of a given narrative will have both a horizontal and vertical dimension. The patterns run in both directions.[3] This interaction of the vertical and the horizontal is possible—or inevitable—because an element in one level may have a correlation with another element in its own level or with elements in one or more other levels.[4] We shall also see that a given element may belong to more than one level at the same time, and that an element may find its correlate in a paradigm that extends all of the way out of the narrative into the corpus or genre to which the narrative belongs.

At this stage an eclectic definition of narrative may be offered as a starting point for identifying the various levels. A narrative is a *discourse* related by *someone* which integrates into a *story* a meaningful, and not just chronological, *succession* or series of events (real or fictitious) which are of human interest.[5] The scheme that I have chosen (there are other ways of doing it) involves the following levels. Narrative at the *story* level is objective statement creating a world of events and persons who are real from the viewpoint of that created world. Story is typically characterized, among other ways, by the use of the third person and of the aorist (past) and pluperfect tenses. The *discourse* level of narrative is subjective articulation, a word spoken by a narrator to a hearer.[6]

The story level can be further analyzed into the sequential and *actantiel* levels. A third level, the indicial, will sometimes belong to the story and sometimes to the discourse.[7] All of these levels will be further defined and illustrated as the chapter progresses. But before moving to that discussion I should like to take up here a certain disputed point.

Eugenio Donato argues that structuralists agree in treating literature as a type of writing from which the subject of articulation has been eliminated. It is his view that structuralists especially oppose the subject of phenomenological thought, which is the same as the Cartesian subject.[8] To this I would make three responses: (1) Our discussion has already shown that all structuralists do not reject subjective articulation in literature, the level of discourse. (2) The subject of phenomenological thought—at least some of it —is not the abstract ego of the Cartesian "I think." It is rather the self which is regained and actualized by means of hermeneutical reflection on and appropriation of the work, acts, and symbols created by the culture through man's effort to exist.[9] (3) In any case I agree with the tendency of Georges Poulet's thought that a work is not to be understood exhaustively as the interdependence of objective levels or structures. If the subjective element is not to be found in the psychology of the author, there is, nevertheless, a certain inherent organizational power at work in the text itself[10] (see my discussion of the narrator or incarnate author in Chapter III).

The sequential level is composed of those elements—sequential functions—which keep the story moving. It is in a sense the heart of the syntagm. There are various ways of grasping, expressing, and formalizing the sequential level, several of which will be used in explicating Mark. It should be kept in mind that when a structural model is used—either at this level or at some other—then Mark is being displayed as a realization of *littérarité*.

The first major step in this section will be to deal with the Markan syntagm as a whole. Let us say, using Barthes's categories, that Mark is a sequence composed of three cardinal (or sequential) functions which open, maintain, and close the narrative, the narrative being understood as a possibility or an uncertainty. Each of these functions has both a logical and a chronological connection with the other cardinal functions (a catalysis on the other hand has only a chronological function and separates two moments of the story). The meaning of each is its capacity to enter into a correlation with the others, and the correlate of a sequential function will usually be on the same level, on the syntagmatic axis. It is always possible to name a sequence—fraud, treason, struggle, agreement, seduction, etc.—and this name is closely tied to the logic which holds the sequence together.[11] Perhaps the best name for the Markan sequence in its totality is conflict.

Sequential functions may be of varying magnitude; they may be superior or inferior to a sentence, and these functions may be separated from each other. They will not necessarily coincide with traditional narrative units—actions, scenes, paragraphs, dialogues, etc.[12] When we consider the Markan syntagm as a whole, each of the three major functions will comprise a rather lengthy segment of the text. But when we begin to analyze or dismember the syntagm, items which had only been elements in the functions of the whole syntagm will become sequences and functions in their own right.

As we get into the Markan narrative we may recall Marxsen's position that Mark consolidates history into one point (to be discussed more fully later). I argued in the last chapter that for Mark history or historical existence occurs in a chronological continuum. Starobinski also refers to unfolding Mark's internal temporality but considers this a synchronic analysis and not a diachronic one, for the latter would be to relate Mark to its own time.[13] Marxsen denies internal temporality but is concerned about Mark's diachronic relation to its own time. The question of internal temporality will have to be raised again when we discuss the relationships among the various narrative levels of Mark and the logic growing out of these relationships. But at least at the sequential level Mark observes the passage of time. Although he does often employ the historic present tense (the use of the present to refer to the past), he freely utilizes the future tense and both the imperfect and aorist tenses with all sorts of verbs and in connection with all sorts of characters.

Now where are we to make the cuts that constitute the three cardinal functions? Where does the opening of the narrative end and the maintaining function begin? Clearly we are still in the opening through the baptism (1:9–11). God initiates a special relationship with Jesus (beloved Son), but we are uncertain as to what he will do with this or what it will mean for the world. The transition to the maintaining function might be seen in the temptation, for here we see that Jesus' special status produces some kind of conflict. But it is a conflict within Jesus; we still do not know how his status will affect the world of men. There is as yet no historical or interpersonal conflict. The implication of 3:27 is that Jesus was successful in the intra-personal conflict, and as God had initiated something with Jesus in the baptism, so Jesus in 1:14–15 initiates something with man. He announces that a new time has come and begins to call men into a new community (1:16–20).

But in 1:21–27 Jesus is opposed by the demonic which inhabits and possesses the human. Now, therefore, we know that his mission is arousing opposition in the world. The uncertainty about the effect of the new initiative has been dispelled, and we know that the narrative is going to be maintained. It will not die for lack of conflict. Thus the maintaining function begins with the exorcism story in 1:21–27.

Throughout a large portion of the text the narrative is maintained by the opposition to Jesus as proclaimer of the kingdom and the bringer of life-salvation. He is opposed in various ways by the Jewish authorities, the demons, his disciples, and the crowds, and his death is anticipated early (2:20; 3:6). Jesus, however, continues the struggle, defends himself, and rides into Jerusalem as a victor. He acts authoritatively in the temple and defeats his opponents in debate (12).

Does not the closing begin at 14:46—"And they laid hands on him and seized him"? After this he is immediately abandoned by all, and he no longer either initiates or defends. The conflict is over: he is killed. But that is penultimate for he is raised: the tomb is empty. The global picture in Mark is: (1) opening: the kingdom is inaugurated; (2) maintaining: there is conflict between the old world and the new world of the kingdom; (3) closing: the representative of the kingdom is apparently defeated but is ultimately victorious. Death and resurrection are explicit in the closing. They have been transformed into opposition and defense in the middle function. Life is primary in the opening, but death (opposition) is suggested by the temptation. Thus the opposition death/resurrection is the fundamental kernel out of which the narrative as a whole develops. This is formalized in figure #9, syntagm 1.

FIGURE #9

Syntagm ⟶

		1. opening	2. maintaining	3. closing	
1	Mark	God and Jesus initiate the kingdom	conflict between Jesus (the kingdom) and Jesus' opponents	Jesus' death	Jesus' resurrection
2	1:1–8:26	God and Jesus initiate the kingdom	the conflict with opponents	the Pharisees request a sign, and the disciples are hardhearted and imperceptive	the healing of the blind man at Bethsaida
3	8:27–16:8	Jesus raises the question of his identity with his disciples	he is misunderstood by them and opposed by the Jewish authorities	Jesus' death	Jesus' resurrection
4	8:31 9:31 10:33–34	Jesus raises the question of his identity	he is to be rejected and condemned	he will be killed	he will rise from the dead
5	10:32–52	Jesus walks ahead of his disciples and teaches them about his coming suffering in Jerusalem	the disciples are afraid and imperceptive: James and John ask for first place	James and John are told that they will die	blind Bartimaeus has his sight restored
6	12–16	Jesus tells the parable of The Wicked Tenants	the Jewish authorities want to arrest him and make repeated efforts to entrap and beguile him	they succeed in killing Jesus	parousia (13) - - - - - - - resurrection (16)

7	13	the disciples initiate a discourse, and Jesus responds	the disciples will be tested: need for discernment	threat of death to disciples	return of Son of Man
8	14:3–9	a woman anoints Jesus with ointment	she is criticized	the anointing is associated with Jesus' death	such a response to his death generates preaching
9	5:21–24,35–43	Jairus requests help from Jesus to which Jesus responds	doubt is expressed about Jesus' powers	the child is dead or apparently so	Jesus' word restores her (resurrection language)
10	7	the Pharisees challenge the cultic purity of Jesus' disciples	controversy about the Scripture	the disciples fail to understand the true nature of good and evil	the Syrophoe-necian woman is perceptive; the deaf mute is healed
11	6:30–52	Jesus takes the disciples to a lonely place and is followed by a crowd	the disciples have doubts about how the crowd can be fed	the crowd is hungry	Jesus feeds them
12	2:1–12	the paralytic's friends make their way to Jesus	Jesus pronounces the paralytic forgiven and is tacitly accused of blasphemy	guilt and lameness of the paralytic	the word of forgiveness and healing
13	2:23–27	the disciples pluck grain on the sabbath	the Pharisees attack Jesus		Jesus claims messianic authority over the sabbath
14	6:45–52	Jesus puts the disciples in a boat	they are afraid	they misunder-stand and are hard of heart	Jesus' word of encouragement
15	8:13–26	Jesus leaves the Pharisees and departs with the disciples in a boat	there is a discussion about bread	the disciples lack understanding	the blind man is given his sight
16	1:21–28	Jesus enters a synagogue	a demon opposes him	the demon convulsed the man	Jesus exorcises the demon, and his fame spreads
17	5:1–20	Jesus arrives in Gerasa	the demons oppose him	swine are killed ; the local people are hostile	the demoniac is restored and wants to follow Jesus
18	9:16–27	Jesus arrives and a man requests healing help for his son	doubt is expressed about Jesus' power, and the demon convulses the boy	the boy is left as if dead	Jesus' word and action raise the boy
19	1:2–8 6:17–29 9:9–13	John announces the coming of the mightier one and makes a moral demand	he is imprisoned by Herod and hated by Herodias	John is beheaded	as Elijah returned he is the restorer of all
20	15:1–39	the Jewish leaders bring Jesus to Pilate	Pilate (Roman governor) questions him and delivers him to execution	Jesus is killed	the veil of the temple is rent and the Roman cen-turion confesses faith in Jesus as Son of God.

† Paradigm

A biographical plot presents a birth to death scheme by straightening out the circular view of time found in fertility myths. What was regarded in the myth as necessary for every new lease on life (like the new year)—the victory of fertility (life) over sterility (death)—is projected both backward and forward, is given a cosmic dimension, and becomes the beginning and end of the whole series. The didactic element in fiction also derives from myth. The romantic plot, whose chief motif is the desire for consummation, is a transformation of the ritual which went along with the myth and attempted to realize the latter in human life.[14]

Mark combines both of these plot motifs. It displays a truncated (no birth) biographical pattern which projects the victory of life both backward and forward cosmically—to the opening of the heavens at the baptism and to the expected return of the Son of Man from heaven in the eschatological future. The life/death theme is presented didactically as well as narratively, and the eschatological future is, of course, presented didactically (13). The romantic motif is seen in the desire to consummate or realize the kingdom or life (1:14–15; 10:15, 17, 24–27) through Jesus' death (10:45; 15:37–39) which is ritually appropriated (14:22–25). Thus Mark is a fusion of the mythic-biographical with the ritual-romantic, in which the myth and ritual are still showing.

Barthes[15] suggests that there can be more than one intelligible view of how a sequence is composed. We see that this is true when we take up the model used by Claude Bremond and the sequential functions as he defines and denominates them. Recall that when we were using Barthes's concept of cardinal (sequential) functions, the uncertainty as to how the opening initiative would be received was dispelled by a conflict which began at 1:21. This conflict was

FIGURE #10

opening up of possibility or virtuality	possibility actualized in a process of amelioration	a goal is reached or a goal is not reached
	or it is not actualized	
opening up of possibility or virtuality	possibility actualized in a process of degradation	a goal is reached or a goal is not reached
	or it is not actualized	

really over at 14:46. For Bremond the three sequential functions are: (1) A possibility is opened up, virtuality is created, a goal is brought into view. (2) The author can then actualize the possibility in a process or let it remain in a state of virtuality. (3) If he chooses to actualize the process, he can then have it reach a goal or simply stop in the course of development. The process can be one either of amelioration or degradation, and all of the possible basic narratives are complications of these three functions portrayed in the form of amelioration or degradation.[16] The fundamental possibilities are represented in a purely formal way in figure #10.

In Mark a new possibility for the relation between God and man is raised by the opening of the heavens at the baptism and by the suggested defeat of Satan in the temptation (see 3:27). But the very appearance of Satan suggests also the possibility of opposition. Where does the second function—and Mark does choose to actualize a process—begin? Does 1:14–15 belong to the first or second function? John the Baptist belongs to 1:1–13, but his ministry is over in 1:14. Also Jesus' messianic status is explicit (for the reader) in 1:1–13 but not in 1:14–15, and we are in a more mythological world in the prologue than we are in the succeeding verses. Mark 1:14–15 is probably more closely related to the call of disciples in 1:16–20 than to the prologue. Therefore, I take 1:14–15 to be the beginning of the process of amelioration. The process is actualized by preaching because for Mark Jesus' word is effective (1:22; 1:41; 2:5, 11; 5:8, 13, 41–42; 7:34; 9:25–26). Intertwined with the process of amelioration is a process of degradation = opposition-to-Jesus manifested in the hostility of the Jewish leaders and in the misunderstanding of the disciples. This dual process is continued until an (apparent) goal is reached (15:37)—and then reversed. Mark as projected onto Bremond's model may be seen in figure #11, but the implications of this will be discussed further below when the Markan syntagm is subjected to a finer analysis.

FIGURE #11

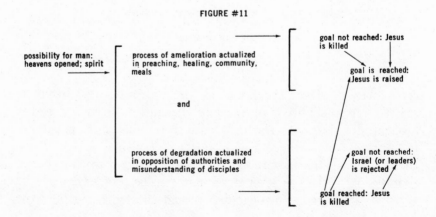

The third and last model to be used in analyzing the Markan sequence as a whole will be that of the tests which a hero must undergo as he seeks to make good a loss or lack of which an individual or a community is the victim. As the hero leaves in search of the missing benefit he is separated from the community of his origin (disjunction) and must pass through certain tests: (1) A *qualifying* test provides him with the necessary help to confront the following test. (2) In the course of the *principal* test he recovers the missing benefit. (3) During the *glorifying* test he must be recognized as a hero by his own with whom he is rejoined (conjunction), and the lack is finally liquidated. Sometimes a test turns out to be a defeat and thus must be begun again.[17] This is graphically represented in figure #12.

FIGURE #12

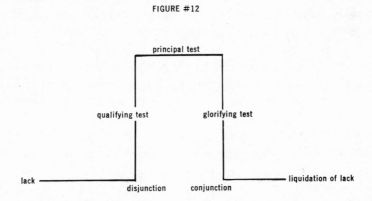

The Markan narrative early informs us of a lack. John's preaching, looking to the future (1:7–8), suggests that the Holy Spirit is absent from Israel and the time is empty and needs to be filled (see 1:15) by the kingdom. When the story begins Jesus has evidently already experienced a certain severance from his family and community (3:21, 31–35), but when he comes to be baptized he is associated with the crowd that throngs around John (1:5). Jesus' qualifying test is in two parts which are separated by a disjunction. He is established as God's Son and given the Holy Spirit, following upon which he is driven into the wilderness (disjunction)

where he is victorious over Satan. Jesus, however, does not remain in disjunction until after the glorifying test. He rather begins to form a new community in connection with which he experiences a number of disjunctions and conjunctions, some complete (6:7, 30) and some partial (5:37; 6:1).

The principal test is at Caesarea Philippi where he retains and refuses to relinquish the kind of messiahship (suffering) which alone can give life (8:31–37). There is a certain fusion of the glorifying test with the principal test inasmuch as the disciples recognize Jesus as messiah at Caesarea Philippi, but this is an inadequate recognition. We must also say that in some sense Jesus did not "pass" the principal test because he undergoes the same kind of struggle with regard to suffering in Gethsemane (14:32–36), but this time his resolve is unshakable.

The glorifying test is the transfiguration (9:2–13) where Jesus' true nature is revealed but not really grasped. Prior to this test there is a disjunction from the main body of disciples (he takes only three upon the mountain), and following it there is a conjunction (9:14). Since the true and full nature of his sonship is not grasped in this glorifying test, there must be another, the resurrection. Again, prior to the resurrection there has been a disjunction (14:50), and subsequent to it a conjunction is implied (16:7). But even if this conjunction with the disciples is fulfilled all men will not recognize Jesus for who he is; therefore a third glorifying test—the parousia—is projected into the future, at which time man's lack will be fully liquidated. Between the resurrection and the parousia disciples will be tested to see if they are truly following the suffering Son of Man.

The question is often raised as to whether the transfiguration points to the parousia[18] or to the resurrection,[19] but this is, I think, not the right way to put the question. It does not really point to or anticipate either one of them. They all three mean the same thing because they are synonymous correlates in the paradigm "glorifying test." They have been dispersed at various points in the syntagm because of the needs of the latter. The same thing is true in principle for Caesarea Philippi and Gethsemane. The way in which Mark is projected onto the test model, minus a few details, can be seen in figure #13.

FIGURE #13

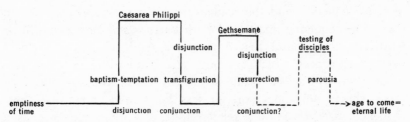

It would be appropriate at this point to note Vielhauer's argument that in Mark Jesus became Son of God in a three-stage process and that this process corresponds to an old Egyptian ceremonial for the deification of the king:

(1) At the baptism Jesus is adopted and installed as Son: the king receives divine attributes from his heavenly father.

(2) At the transfiguration Jesus is revealed as Son: the deified king is presented to the circle of the gods.

(3) The centurion confesses Jesus as Son in the fully Christian sense: lordship is conferred upon the king and he is enthroned.[20]

Whether or not this scheme has a direct or indirect historical connection with the Egyptian enthronement ceremonial—and it may —it certainly has the closest kind of connection with what we have seen to be the Markan sequence level, and also a structural connection with the Egyptian scheme. It has the least close connection with Mark as projected onto the test model. The first Son of God passage (baptism) coincides with the qualifying test, but there is no correlate for the principal test (Caesarea Philippi). Rather the second and third Son of God passages correspond to two elements in the glorifying test paradigm—the transfiguration and the centurion's confession (the centurion's confession, as we shall see, belongs in the same paradigm with the transfiguration and the resurrection). With regard to the other two models that we used, in both cases the three Son of God passages fit respectively into the three primary sequential functions. The baptism opens the narrative and creates possibility. The transfiguration maintains the process, and there is a real sense in which the centurion's confession is a closing function. This relating of events to christological titles is an anticipation of the whole matter of the vertical relationship of levels which will be more systematically discussed later.

We turn now to a finer analysis or dismemberment of the Markan sequence, and the reader is invited to keep figure #9 in view. The sequential models of both Barthes and Bremond will be used. On the ground that a narrative tends to repeat itself in parallel sequences which are both alike and different from each other,[21] we will select certain sequences within Mark—some relatively short and some more or less long—and show that these sequences are structurally related to the Markan sequence as a whole; that is, these sequences not only repeat each other but they recapitulate the totality of Mark. By paralleling the Markan sequence with certain constituent sequences we will build a grid of syntagms and paradigms which will display the deep structure (thus far we have been dealing primarily with the surface sequential structure of Mark) of the Gospel's sequence[22] and manifest the correlation of meaning between the full Markan sequence and its component sequences.[23]

Cornford points out that the typical Aristophanic comedy is divided into two parts by an event called the parabasis. At this juncture the chorus moves across the orchestra and addresses the audience directly. Prior to the parabasis is the agon: a fierce verbal contest, comparable to a duel, in which the hero is attacked or even threatened with death and is put on his defense, but he wins by argument. Or the agon may be after the parabasis or there may be one both before and after. In any case, as we saw in Chapter II, the hero's final victory or "resurrection" is celebrated at the end.[24]

In Mark Jesus' question about his identity at Caesarea Philippi (8:27–29) and Peter's reply—"You are the Christ"—correspond not in content but formally to the parabasis. This scene divides Mark into two parts and the audience is being addressed; that is, this pericope is discourse as well as story (the reason for saying this will be given later). The agon prior to Caesarea Philippi, though hinting at death, is chiefly verbal, and is primarily a conflict between Jesus and the Jewish authorities. The tension between Jesus and his disciples, however, has also emerged prior to Caesarea Philippi so that the death operation in syntagm 2 (Mark 1:1–8:26) of figure #9 is the hardheartedness and imperception of the disciples while the resurrection operation is the restoration of sight to the blind man (8:22–26). In syntagm 3 (Mark 8:27–16:8) the controversy with the disciples has become at least as prominent as that with the Jewish authorities. Throughout the conflict sections Jesus makes telling and incisive verbal defenses, but the overall movement of the action is against him.

Since the attack against the hero in the second paradigm is itself a transformation of death, sometimes a "second" death will hardly appear in paradigm 3. We might also observe that, since a logic governs a sequence, sometimes elements in a syntagm are slightly rearranged to express better the logic which is emerging in the grid, as whole and parts react upon each other. For example in syntagm 12 the healed man's lameness is mentioned and his guilt implied, and Jesus' forgiving word is spoken before the scribes condemn Jesus. In the syntagm which represents Mark as a whole Jesus is the central figure in all three functions. But in the other syntagms different characters are often the subject or object of the action in the different functions. This is no flaw in the scheme because at this level we are concerned about the structural relationship of *actions* or functions, not about the characters or their relationship to actions. Even in a comic play as a whole the action is not always unified by a single character. In Aristophanes' *Plutus,* for example, Plutus is the victor in the final comos, but an associate of his wins the first agon.

The reasons for the structuring of the individual syntagms are, I think, fairly obvious, but a few of them warrant some comment. With reference to syntagms 12–17 we might observe that James Robinson has maintained that in Mark there is a close relationship between the cosmic struggle inaugurated at the baptism, the exorcisms, and Jesus' debates with his opponents; the debates continue the cosmic struggle.[25] The Jewish authorities are hostile and the disciples uncomprehending. Best opposes Robinson's position, arguing that the exorcisms and the debates are independent. The demonic in Mark is not related to that kind of evil which separates man from God but rather to impersonal forms of evil. At Caesarea Philippi Satan does not indwell or use Peter but rather Peter is behaving in the manner of Satan (surely a very fine distinction). Nor does Mark indicate that demonic power prevents understanding.[26]

But even Best admits that in the temptation Satan tempts to moral evil.[27] Surely, structurally speaking, *the* temptation is a cardinal function which bears fruit in the "temptations" at Caesarea Philippi and in Gethsemane. Moreover, in Mark 4:15 Satan takes away the proclaimed word in a context in which the matter of hearing with understanding is of prime importance (4:9, 21–25). Finally figure #9 shows that the debates with the Jewish authorities and with the disciples and the exorcisms are all transformations of the same structure. Surely Robinson has the better of the argument.

As for syntagm 19, it has been stated that the story of John's execution (6:16–29) is the only narrative in Mark which is not in some way about Jesus.[28] There is a certain literal and obvious sense in which this is a true statement. But there is a deeper sense in which it is not true. One can hardly doubt that the structure which generated Mark is responsible for the presence of the story of John's execution. Without that episode John's story would be incomplete. But with it John's story in the Gospel of Mark fits very neatly into our three cardinal functions: (1) John announces the coming of the mightier one (1:8) which is accompanied by a moral demand (1:4; 6:18) (opening). (2) He is imprisoned and opposed (6:17, 19) maintaining). (3) He is killed (6:27) but as the Elijah returned who restores all things he is a resurrected one (9:9–13) (closing). Thus in Mark John's story and Jesus' are transformations of the same structure.

In Figure #9, the elements in the opening paradigm are typically actions. Occasionally a sequence begins with the statement of a condition, but most characteristically it begins with an initiating action. Mark is globally a narrative about people—or God—acting, not one about people being acted upon (unless that is the result of someone else's action). God initiates a relationship with Jesus, and Jesus initiates the process of the kingdom. He raises with the disciples the question of his identity, provokes the Jewish leaders with the parable of The Wicked Tenants, takes his disciples to a lonely place, puts them on a boat, leads them to Jerusalem, enters a synagogue, etc. A woman anoints him with ointment, Jairus seeks his help, four men unroof a house to get their paralytic friend to his feet, his enemies plot his death and take him before Pilate. Initiating action is one of the elements in the Markan semantic micro-universe.

If we read the full paradigms from left to right the elemental logic that governs Mark's narrative is that initiating action arouses a reaction—hostility, incomprehension, doubt, questioning—which issues in death and resurrection.

As we consider the death and resurrection sub-paradigms of the closing paradigm let us recall that all the elements of a paradigm are drawn from the same pool, are correlates of each other, and in some way interpret each other. In the Markan narrative Jesus literally dies, and it is suggested that he literally rose from the dead. Now what is the relationship of the other elements in the two respective paradigms to the "historical" event of Jesus' death and resurrection? Or how does the Markan narrative sequence in light of its intersecting paradigms interpret death and resurrection (and let us not forget that one brings a signified to the signifier and that constructing a structure is fabricating a meaning)? I would suggest first of all that the other elements are not merely allegorical ciphers or pointers to death and resurrection. They do not simply mean death and resurrection expressed in other terms. These elements are symbols of death and resurrection. They both mean and are something in themselves and also point to the death and resurrection in which they participate and which they make present to the extent that they become language event. Beyond this I expect that the "logics" of the death and resurrection paradigms are not quite the same.

Jesus died, and we will die. We know that we will die, and we know that others die, but we cannot fully enter into the death of another or fully experience our own until it happens. But we know something about death when we are involved in its symbols, its paradigmatic correlates. It is death to be hostile or uncomprehending and hard of heart before a new possibility of life that threatens to turn everything old upside down. It is death to want—to need—visible proof that the new is really here. We know death in the guilt that separates from God and in illness that saps our vital powers and in hunger that makes us tremble. To be caught in a religious scrupulosity that denies the needs of everyday life is death. Man dies when he is alienated from himself and from society as if by a power beyond himself. But all of this is not quite death; it does not exhaust it, for we must still die. Death is a fact of historical existence.

But if the resurrection is not exhausted by its symbols, it is not transcended by a historical event, the resurrection. We do not experience the resurrection of Jesus itself in or as historical event. Jesus' resurrection may be considered a trans-historical reality, a position which I attempted to explicate and defend earlier,[29] and which I think I would still stick by. This trans-historical reality is experienced only by engagement in the symbols of the resurrection; the resurrection "occurs" only in and through these symbols, and the symbols are not transcended by a historical resurrection. Thus we could say that the symbols of a death are transcended by the event (history) of death, but the history of death is transcended by the symbols of the resurrection.

The resurrection is the word of Jesus, continued in the preaching of the church, which brings forgiveness, sight, understanding, healing, and freedom from demonic possession. It is the faith which knows Jesus as Son of God–Son of Man, as the one who feeds and gives deliverance from the strangling power of ritual over everyday vitalities.

This statement of the meaning of death/resurrection is not outrageous theological eisegesis but an interpretation of the paradigms constructed from the sequence of the Markan story.

At this point I should like to give a further analysis of the Markan narrative as represented in figure #11. One way in which the simplest narrative—one process line—can be complicated is by adding a second process, a step which Bremond calls enclave.[30] Figure #11 already shows that Mark does this. The enclave is developed because the process of amelioration needs the process of degradation in order to attain its goal; the process of degradation is the means.[31] In Markan terms Jesus' saving initiative needs the opposition of the Pharisees and the disciples because life comes through death.

Jesus begins as the one who dispenses amelioration, but the impediments placed in his way finally reduce him to death, that is, to one who needs amelioration. This is given so that once more, through the resurrection, Jesus becomes the bestower of amelioration. This follows the typical pattern of a hero suffering as the result of a "natural" relationship which imposes a duty upon him. If he fulfills the duty, then his act becomes a meritorious sacrifice which deserves a reward and produces credit.[32] Hence in Mark Jesus suffers because he is an obedient son (1:11; 14:36) with the result that he is resurrected and makes credit available for others (10:45).

The process of amelioration is the process of eliminating the impediments or obstacles, which, according to Bremond,[33] can be accomplished in one of two ways: (1) The protagonist may act peacefully and try to persuade the adversary to cease his opposition and thus try to make him an ally. In Mark we see this both in the debates with the Pharisees and in the discussions with the disciples. (2) There may be a hostile effort to render the adversary incapable of opposition. In Mark there is a suggestion that God does, or will do, this (12:9–11).

But more profoundly Mark dialectically fuses the two means of "elimination." Very much as in 1 Corinthians 1 the opponent of Jesus (or God) must be brought to nothing so that there can be new life. The old self which opposes the gospel must die in order that a new self might be born (8:34–36; 10:15, 42–45) and become an ally—a disciple—of Jesus.

The process of degradation can come from the initiative, or at least from the character, of responsible agents or it can originate in some other way.[34] For Mark the origin of the process of degradation is seen dialectically in two ways. On the one hand those who put Jesus to death act on their own volition (3:6; 12:12; 14:1–2; 15:1), yet it is a divine necessity that Jesus must die (8:31; 14:21). Jesus' words are taken as needing to be explained so that the disciples could not expect to understand without special explanations (4:10–12, 34). But even when Jesus gives explanations or acts in a way whose meaning should be self-evident, they still do not understand and are blamed for being hardhearted (6:52; 7:14–18; 8:17–21; 9:10, 32; 10:26–27). Thus Jesus' death is both a part of the divine necessity and the "fault" of man.

There is a flaw in the process of degradation if men choose a course of action opposed to their goal.[35] This is precisely what the Jewish leaders do. Their goal is to maintain the law (2:1–3:6; 7:1–6)—a secured relationship with God—and their safe position both with the people and with Rome (11:18, 32; 14:1–2; 15:1–2). Their goal is a "place" in the world at their own disposal. The means is to get rid of Jesus whom they see as threatening their place, and they appear to have achieved the goal when they succeed in having Jesus killed. They think that killing Jesus is the equivalent of their goal, but it turns out to be a means which destroys their goal. By achieving the "goal" of killing Jesus they defeat their own purpose, shatter their real goal of having a place (or relationship) which they can control (12:9), and bring about the achievement of Jesus' goal —life, resurrection—for only by dying could he live (8:31–37). The effort of the Jewish leaders has been reversed because God has chosen the "stone" which they rejected (12:10–11). God reverses man's effort to secure his position: he is expelled from the Vineyard (12:9–11).

A second method of complicating the simple narrative process is by what Bremond calls bracketing.[36] Since Mark uses both enclave and bracketing, the latter is the particular way in which he relates the two processes—amelioration and degradation—in the operation of the enclave. Bracketing is presenting the same series of events as simultaneously amelioration and degradation by having two (or more) agents with different (opposed) interests involved in and affected by these events. The degradation of the fate of one coincides with the amelioration of the fate of the other.[37] This has already been suggested by figure #11. The degradation of Jesus' fate in his death is the (apparent) amelioration of his opponents' fate while the amelioration of his fate in his resurrection is the (apparent?) degradation of the fate of the opposition.

Two points of view are at play among the characters: that of Jesus on the one hand and that of the Jewish leaders (or the disciples) on the other. The process of opposition to Jesus is a degradation from the standpoint of Jesus (and of Mark), but from the Pharisees' standpoint Jesus' mission to bring the kingdom is a degradation of the law (man's relation to God) and of their security. For the disciples Jesus' view of messiahship evidently degrades that concept. What I am calling the process of degradation displays, selectively, the interpretation which Jesus' opponents make of his actions and mission—their opposition to him. The degradation process is an impediment to Jesus' process of amelioration, but it happens because the Pharisees and disciples interpret Jesus' process of amelioration as one of degradation. Figure #14 represents an elaboration of Figure #11. The symbol *vs.* stands for the opposing points of view. The question at issue is whether man's relationship with God depends on the unexpected manifestations of the kingdom or on maintaining the order of the established religious culture.

FIGURE #14

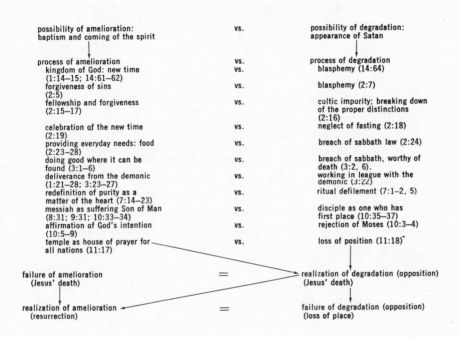

The *actantiel* level is composed of *actants*. An *actant* is not a character but is a function, role, or status whose quality is to be the subject of or participant in a constant action. The actant is perhaps usually a personal character, but it may be an object, institution, feeling, disposition, condition, etc. Grammatically it corresponds to the present participle. A story may have any number of characters but no more than six actants, although it may have fewer. This means that one actant may be represented in several characters and that one character may fulfill more than one actant. According to the *actantiel* scheme widely held in structural analysis a subject (S) desires to possess an object (O) or to communicate it to a recipient (R), the object proceeding from an ordainer (Or). In this effort the subject may be aided by a helper (H) or impeded by an opponent (Op).[38]

In figure #15 this model is presented graphically in order to show the relationship between the actants and is illustrated in con-

FIGURE #15

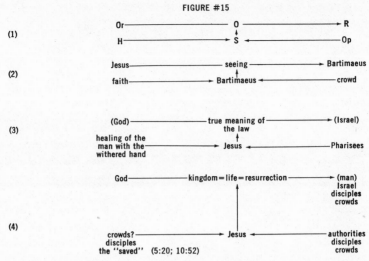

nection with two Markan pericopes. Then Mark as a whole is projected onto the model. In the healing of blind Bartimaeus (10:46–52) the blind beggar wants to receive his sight from Jesus. He is impeded in his effort by the crowd but helped by his faith, and Jesus grants his request. Bartimaeus is successful in his effort and thus is both subject and recipient. In Mark 3:1–6 Jesus wants to communicate to man or Israel (the implied recipient)—to reestablish— the true meaning of the law. He is opposed by the Pharisees and aided by the healing of the man with the withered hand. God is the implied ordainer. The tacit view of the Pharisees is that one must choose one of the members from the opposition to-do-on-the-sabbath/ not-to-do-on-the-sabbath, while the view that Jesus is trying to establish is that one must choose between the two alternatives to-do-good/to-do-evil.[39]

In the Gospel of Mark globally Jesus wants to communicate the kindom = life, which comes from God, to man-Israel-disciples-crowd. He is impeded (yet as we have seen ironically helped) by the authorities and the disciples and the crowds. Those whom he would help ironically oppose him. In certain ways the crowds and disciples also help him in a nonironical way.

We must now consider each of the actants individually. The *actantiel* object, the kingdom, was sufficiently discussed in Chapter III, section B, under the rubric of Mark's understanding of historical existence. To recapitulate in summary fashion: the kingdom is the possibility of gaining life through death.

We turn then to the subject, Jesus. Mark is concerned both with who Jesus is and what he does, and we observe that the former question is raised by the latter. The Pharisees ask why Jesus does or allows certain things. They want to know why he eats with tax collectors and sinners (2:16), why his disciples do not fast (2:18), and why his disciples pluck grain on the sabbath (2:24). In each case Jesus answers as if they had asked "who are you?" for he replies by telling them who he is: I am the physician, the bridegroom, the Son of Man who is lord of the sabbath.[40]

Thus the note of authority, an important one for Mark, is sounded. Authority connotes both right and power,[41] and Jesus exercises this authority by calling disciples, his word being effective like the word of God in the Old Testament (Ps. 33:9; Isa. 55:10–11).[42] Jesus' authority is manifested both in his teaching and in his mighty acts, and his exorcisms are seen as evidence for the authority of his teaching (1:21, 22, 27; 2:13; 6:2, 6, 7; 10:1).[43] As the man of authority Jesus is the singular one who stands over against all sorts of crowds, including the disciples whom he has called (1:35; 4:35–5:21; 10:32).[44] Yet Jesus also plays the role of the eiron, in fact a kind of double eiron—a hero who makes himself out as worse or less or other than he is.[45] As a man of questionable religious attainments he turns the tables on the "authorities" by his authoritative answers; he pronounces sins forgiven and the sabbath set aside. But despite these claims of authority he lets events sweep him away. When he is arrested, he does not resist, and before Pilate he is quite passive.

Jesus does not assert authority for its own sake. In fact, he who would be ruler must be servant of all (10:42–45). Jesus' authority is the power to communicate—teaching, healing, forgiveness—to others. But above all he communicates himself, and here the meal "code" is very important.

"Code" refers to a pattern or organization of similar functions.[46] In Mark the meal-functions are sufficiently constant and important to be taken up into the actant which Jesus fulfills. In the two feeding miracles Jesus provides the elements of the meal (and by the language used [compare 6:41; 8:6; 14:22] anticipates the final meal). The food is the medium of the fellowship or community, that in which the members participate in common. Jesus also is one of the participants in the fellowship; he is joined to the others by common participation, and he interprets his presence as that of the physician who heals the sinful (2:15–17). It is the meal—the vehicle of common participation—that makes this particular kind of presence possible. Finally the meal is the symbolic means whereby he actually conveys himself to others and is received by them (14:22–25). Thus Jesus as the *actantiel* subject is the self-communicating one.

Now in Mark there is a very close relationship between Jesus and the kingdom. Recall from our analysis of the Markan sequence (figure #9) that Jesus' initiation of the kingdom by his preaching and his raising the question of his identity belong to the same paradigm; they are correlates of each other. The proclamation of the new time and the challenge to discern who Jesus is put man in the same critical situation. Jesus proclaims the kindom of God (1:14–15) as the only possible—and therefore necessary—means of salvation (10:23, 26–27) for man. He also proclaims his (the Son of Man's) death and resurrection as the necessary (8:31; 14:21) means of salvation for man (10:45; 14:22–25). The difficulty of entering the kingdom (10:23) is the same as the difficulty of following in Jesus' way (10:21–22). Thus Jesus must be the vehicle and instrument of that act of God which alone can deliver man from himself (10:23, 25, 27). Therefore, in communicating himself to men he communicates to them the kingdom.

In Mark's Gospel God fulfills the actant ordainer. As we have just observed, the new possibility which Jesus wants to communicate to men comes ultimately from God: the kingdom is God's. Or God is understood as the source of the new possibility of life through death. At the same time God at certain points fulfills the actant opponent. This comes to expression especially in Mark 4. The outsiders do not perceive the meaning of Jesus' parabolic word and receive forgiveness. Thus they remain outside the kingdom. The quotation from Isaiah 6 in Mark 4:12 assures that Jesus' word is understood as God's word. Jesus uses this kind of word *in order to* keep outsiders out. Thus God and his word (Jesus' parabolic word) impede Jesus' desire to communicate the kingdom of God to man. Roland Barthes observes that from the literary standpoint it is very rare and paradoxical that the ordainer should be identical with an opponent.[47]

This literary paradox is the parallel to—or even the grammatical matrix that makes possible—the tension or paradox in Mark's understanding of God and/as his word. This same tension comes to expression in connection with man's encounter with God's word—in connection with the problem of man's understanding it. The problem will be taken up again in discussing the disciples in Mark.

We turn now (or again) to the *actantiel* opponent and will discuss several of the characters who fulfill this actant. But because some characters fulfill more than one actant it would be artificial to attempt to keep the actants entirely separate in discussion.

The crowd seems to belong finally to the actant opponent. Early in the story, however, the crowds are amazed at Jesus' miracles and glorify God (2:12). They question what this new teaching with authority might be (1:27) and seek Jesus out, especially to be healed by him (1:37; 3:10; 6:33, 53–56).

Now what is the meaning of this attitude on the part of the crowd in the early part of the narrative?[48] (1) Some see it as a very low level of insight or hold that the crowd seeks Jesus only for what it can get out of him.[49] (2) Or the crowd's attitude can be interpreted more positively as reflecting the experience of something which made them question their everyday existence and its security. They sense but do not penetrate the authority of Jesus, yet they somehow recognize the presence of God in it.[50] (3) According to Weeden the role of the crowd is to dramatize a positive response to Jesus in vivid contrast with the reaction of the Jewish authorities.[51]

But I think that two things must be said about Weeden's view: He does not take sufficient account of the action of the crowd in the closing scenes of the Gospel. According to Weeden, the crowd would have to be responding to a divine man Christ since that is what Mark presents in the first half of the Gospel. But Weeden also holds that Mark opposes the divine man Christology. Thus how could Mark make the crowd's response so almost unequivocally positive?

I believe that the second interpretation above leaves more openness for what transpires in the remainder of the story. Mark indicates in the Caesarea Philippi episode that the crowd does not recognize Jesus as messiah (8:28). However, they hail him as he enters Jerusalem in terms that might imply messiahship (11:8–10). But if it is messiahship that they acknowledge, it is Davidic messiahship, not

Mark's (or Mark's Jesus') interpretation of messiahship. Still in the early days of the Jerusalem period the authorities consider the crowd to be supporters of Jesus (11:18), and the function of 12:37–44 may be to show that the crowd are not enemies.[52]

But the crowd is finally persuaded by the chief priests to press for Jesus' execution (15:11–15). The throng witnessing and accompanying Jesus from time to time throughout the book has been titillated by intimations of the numinous, but it has not learned the way of life through death. The crowd in the end is composed of the vacillating ones. Given Mark's tendency to exculpate Pilate (15:4, 9–10, 12), from the story's standpoint (on the level of human volition) Jesus would hardly have been crucified apart from the pressure of the crowd.

The actant opponent is also represented in the demonic and the demons. The demonic kingdom is at war with the kingdom of God (3:22–27, by implication) and consequently is bent on possessing and destroying man, God's creation (see 10:6). In Mark's narrative the demonic defines itself as that power which turns man to self-division (5:5–9), self-destruction (5:5; 9:17–18, 21–22), and isolation from community (5:2–3). The demons thus oppose Jesus because he has come to bring life and to deliver man from the distortions of his existence. They recognize Jesus as their antagonist, try to hold on to their possession—man—and attempt to control Jesus by naming him (1:24; 3:27; 5:6–10; 9:26). But Jesus overcomes their efforts and delivers men (1:25–26, 34; 3:11–12, 27; 5:8, 13, 15, 20; 9:25–27).

To the actant opponent also belong the Jewish authorities. As we have observed, it is a part of Mark's discourse that Jesus dies by divine necessity, and the opposition of the Pharisees et al. is a means to the end of life through death. But from the standpoint of the authorities' own intention they are Jesus' opponents (14:1–2). As supporters of the religion of law they attack him for bringing the disturbing new time. The Pharisees begin with silent questioning (2:6–7), but Jesus' continued provocative acts unmask them as opponents with the intent to kill (3:6),[53] an intention which they finally realize.

The Pharisees are not only arch antagonists but also alazons, boastful claimants of righteousness, the righteousness of the law (2:15–

17; 7:9–13). As proponents of the law they are attached to that which God originally gave for the life of Israel (see Chapter II). But in their hands it has become a structure which denies life (7:9–13) and demands the death of anyone who questions its unalterable demands (2:23–3:6). So encrusted have the Pharisees and scribes become in this structure that they can no longer recognize the present action of the original lawgiver (3:28–30; 8:11–12). Hence they are no longer alive. In their particular *actantiel* role the authorities are transformations of one of the roles or functions which belonged to the ancient fertility rite lying behind Aristophanic comedy. They are paradigmatic correlates of the spirit of sterility or death which causes the death of the good spirit of life, but this spirit of death is itself the former spirit of life now grown old.[54]

The disciples are intended by Jesus to be helpers. They are appointed to be with him and to be sent out to preach and to exorcise (3:13–15). As a matter of fact, when sent out, they do preach, heal, and cast out demons (6:12–13).[55] But the disciples are much more pervasively opponents of a particular type. As we have already noted the alazon is the comic character who claims higher qualities than he has and seeks advantages that he has not earned; especially does he claim a share, undeserved, in the hero's victory.[56] The disciples turn out to be imperceptive, noncomprehending alazon-opponents.

As a group they debate about who is greatest among them (9:34). James and John request the number one and number two positions in Jesus' time of glory, promising also that they are willing to share his death (10:35–39a). Peter claims that they have all given up everything to follow Jesus (10:28) and insists that he will not abandon or deny him no matter what the others do (14:29, 31); and the others are just as confident (14:31). Weeden sees this self-exaltation and comparing on the part of the disciples as reflecting the kind of discipleship which results from the false divine man Christology which he believes Mark to be combatting.[57] But such behavior by the disciples has a semantic affinity with the role of the alazon-opponent in the *actantiel* structural level of comedy. The latter would be the basis for the historical reference of the disciples' role if in fact their role does reflect Mark's historical situation in the way that Weeden believes.

The disciples, then, claim both virtue and privilege. But they do not understand what is involved in Jesus' conception of the dying-rising Son of Man (9:30–32), and they are called hardhearted and imperceptive (6:52; 8:17–21), language which is used of the Pharisees and outsiders elsewhere (3:5; 4:12). It may be that what the disciples fail to comprehend in 8:21 is that Jesus is the one loaf for Jews and gentiles, as the feeding miracles have shown.[58] The disciples also lack the kind of faith that would make prayer effective (4:40; 9:28–29; 11:22–24). In the end Peter does deny Jesus (14:66–72), Judas betrays him (14:10–11, 43–45), and they all abandon him (14:50).

The element of the disciples' lack of understanding is related to the larger problem of the messianic secret. Norman Petersen has affirmed that while Mark is a subtype of aretalogy the author rejects the notion of Jesus as a divine man in that Jesus' death and resurrection qualify his whole life. The secrecy motif is used to show that the one who is construed as a divine man is really someone else. In Petersen's view the origin of the secrecy motif has yet to be determined.[59]

Probably the problem of the secrecy motif still has to be unraveled. But at least that thread which is the disciples' noncomprehension is closely related to the prophetic notion of Israel's hardheartedness (Isa. 6:9–10; Hos. 5:4; Jer. 7:24; 17:1, 9–10; Ezek. 11:19; 36:26). To the extent that the secrecy motif belongs to Mark's historical situation as a means of combatting heresy it is a historical-theological factor causing a transformation in the comic genre. As historical it is grounded in the more fundamental structure of the *actantiel* level. The secrecy motif (noncomprehension) could find its way in only because of the formal place of the alazon-opponent in the *actantiel* "grammar." It is used to develop the role of the disciples as alazons. The genre-structure provides a "place" for the historical elements.

As is well known, the prevailing view of the messianic secret was for many years that Mark used it in order to reconcile the non-messianic tradition about Jesus with the church's faith in him as messiah. A teacher-prophet known not to be the messiah could be portrayed as such only if he were represented as the secret messiah.[60] In more recent years—to be a bit eclectic—the growing position has been that the tradition was already christologically interpreted, in divine man terms, when it reached Mark, and he used the idea of the secret messiah to give his Gospel a unified point of view and to moderate and to bring the divine man Christology into line with the death/resurrection kerygma. The secrecy motif shows that the one who is apparently the divine man is really someone else.[61] Both of these views use a historical signified in trying to grasp the significance of the messianic secret.

Mark probably did inherit a christologically interpreted Jesus tradition, but it may be questionable whether the messianic secret is to be explained as a/the means of toning down the divine man Christology. In Mark Jesus gives orders not to report the event only in three (1:40–45; 5:21–24, 35–43; 7:31–37) of thirteen miracle stories and in none of the three exorcisms. The secrecy element is primarily in the Markan summaries and not in additions which he made to the tradition,[62] a point of no great importance for structural analysis. Moreover, Vielhauer has trenchantly questioned whether the messianic secret is a unified concept in Mark.[63]

In trying to understand the messianic secret we must consider the following phenomena:

(1) The demons are sometimes ordered to silence with regard to Jesus' identity (1:25, 34; 3:12). The order in 1:25 belongs to the logic of the traditional story (as in 4:39) and is made a part of the messianic secret only by the context of 1:34 and 3:12.[64]

(2) Silence *is* ordered in three, if only three, miracle stories.

(3) Outsiders are prevented from understanding Jesus' word (Mark 4:10–12).

(4) The disciples are not to tell anyone that Jesus is the messiah (8:30).

(5) Jesus' true identity is not to be made known until after the resurrection (9:9).

Now it seems to me that all of these items can be subsumed under one category. Mark is giving an a priori interpretation of the nature of God's revelation. The truth *cannot* be made known until a certain time and unless Jesus' way is followed.[65] An a priori theological interpretation is being given of an existential reality. A second motif may also be at work in at least some of these five items: a *false* view of Jesus' messiahship is not to be spread. W. C. Robinson argues that the demons and the disciples express an identical orthodox Christology and that the point is that his messiahship was not to be announced at all.[66] But on the basis of 8:31–37 Peter's confession was not orthodox from Mark's point of view. As for the demons, we do not know what meaning they gave to the titles which they used of Jesus, but we do know that they used them to try to manipulate him. Mark's Jesus does not avoid altogether the use of messianic titles in public. He uses them in 2:10, 28; 14:61–62. Thus we must look at the other side of Mark's theological a priori.

The secret of the kingdom, which is withheld from the outsiders, is explained to the disciples (4:11, 34), and suffering messiahship is openly expounded to them (8:31, 9:31; 10:33–34), but they do not understand who Jesus is or what he is about (8:17–18; 9:10, 32, 34; 10:35–37). Who he is and what he is doing are still a mystery to them. There is a sense in which the death and resurrection have already happened for them: Jesus has openly predicted their occurrence, and the resurrection paradigm in figure #9, which results from the paralleling of structurally similar sequences, shows that the "resurrection" has occurred in various ways. Thus they should understand, and they are held responsible for their hardhearted imperception (7:18; 8:17–18; 10:42–45). Here Mark is taking, not an a priori look at the situation of giving revelation, but an a posteriori look at man's experience in receiving revelation. The point is the difficulty and unwillingness of appropriating existentially[67]—so that one's existence is reoriented—the meaning of life through death even after the resurrection has "occurred" and has been expounded conceptually through the word. Schuyler Brown argues that Mark distinguished the messianic secret in the strict sense from the secret of the kingdom (4:11). He holds that the secret of the kingdom *is* given to the disciples (4:11) and that it has to do with instruction to the disciples about such things as the nature of sin (7:17–22). But while the secret of the *kingdom* is given to them in 4:11, they still have not grasped Jesus' true *identity* in 4:40, 6:49; 8:17–21, and do not until 8:29.[68] But, as we have seen above, the disciples do not really grasp the secret of Jesus' identity after 8:29, and if they have been given the secret of the kingdom in 4:11, they are not in possession of it in 7:17–18 or 10:26. Thus the situation is the same both with regard to the kingdom and to Jesus' identity: the disciples do not have what has been given to them.

Mark does not make a programmatic distinction between the secret of the kingdom and the messianic secret.[69]

In summary recapituation, Mark is expressing the paradox of the revelation or word of God, or he is looking at it from two different angles: (1) God controls his word and it *cannot* be grasped until the history of salvation in Jesus has been completed. (2) Even when it is revealed, man is resistant to accepting it and is responsible for not doing so. However, in the light of Mark's paralleling, there is always "another resurrection" to come; therefore the disciples are always both before and after the resurrection; the word is both withheld and given; they are both helpless and responsible.[70]

As we have seen, Mark does not consistently prevent Jesus from using messianic titles in public nor does he consistently have Jesus suppress reports of his miracles. With the messianic secret Mark is not so much thematizing a problem in the history of Christology as he is man's situation before the revelation of God: the difficulty of appropriating existentially what is known or sensed intellectually, the crucified Son of Man. It took an existential signified to provide access to the paradox which comes to expression in Mark.

If we consider the disciples, the crowds, and the Jewish authorities from the standpoint of the existential a posteriori, and not the theological a priori, then all three are variations of one signified. The crowds are impressed and amazed but lack commitment and intellectual categories for interpretation. The disciples are informed intellectually but are not reoriented existentially. The authorities sense the possible existential consequences of Jesus' mission (12:12), but they reject his messiahship and act to keep the potential from becoming a reality, in which effort they are ironically overruled. Burkill[71] observes that in 14:62 the public disclosure of Jesus' messiahship breaks through the messianic secret and lights up the darkness of the passion. But that is possibly true only at the discourse level of the narrative, for the readers. It is not true at the story level, for the Jewish leaders do not grasp the revelation.

The recalcitrance of man when considered only from the standpoint of the existential a posteriori may incline one again toward the theological a priori. Only the participation of the Son of Man in the full cosmic movement of salvation can save man. If God will not complete his revelation *until* a certain time, it is nevertheless affirmed that he will complete it. The resurrection paradigm is a rich reservoir: if not at the transfiguration, then at the resurrection; if not at the resurrection, then at the parousia. But why should there have to be a *history* of revelation? Why do men resist it? Eric Voegelin suggests that this is a mystery which cannot be solved.[72] Perhaps it is the impenetrability of this mystery which led Mark to approach the situation of man before the word of God in both an a priori and an a posteriori way at the same time.

The indices which comprise the indicial level have a paradigmatic correlate and refer to a signified, according to Roland Barthes. Their sanction is not *further* along the syntagm but is rather higher.[73] There are two types of indices.

An index proper refers to such as character, sentiment, psychological atmosphere, and philosophical—and I would add theological—concepts. Grammatically it is analogous to an adjective.[74]

What Barthes calls an index is closely akin to Scholes's and Kellogg's concept of illustration or symbol. An illustration does not try to duplicate or reproduce reality; it is rather a selected aspect of reality which, for example, does not display a character as a whole person but as the illustration of a principle which belongs to the ethical or metaphysical realm.[75]

The second kind of index Barthes refers to is information. Information situates the narrative in time and space and roots it in the world.[76] If that is the case, then information may be expanded to include the sociological and psychological and would thus be close to what Scholes and Kellogg call representation. Representation does try to duplicate and reproduce actuality, to reshape and revitalize ways of apprehending the world by mimesis (imitation). It seeks to display a specific but not factual relationship between the real world and the world of narrative. The important thing about a basically representational narrative is that the characters and events might pass for real.[77]

One cannot draw the lines too sharply, but I will in my analysis of Mark be a bit closer to Kellogg and Scholes than to Barthes in placing the ethical and theological under the rubric of index proper or illustration (symbol) and including the psychological and sociological, along with the temporal and geographical notes, under the category of information or representation. When one asserts that an index refers to a signified and that its correlate is paradigmatic, this is to say that the audience is expected to be aware of the frame of reference outside of the narrative to which the index points, and the audience is expected to do some deciphering.[78] This implies that in the indices the author is talking to the audience, that the indicial level belongs to discourse rather than to story, an assertion which Barthes makes.[79] But if a certain reader does not possess the knowledge or awareness to catch the paradigmatic reference of a particular index, then if it functions at all for him, it can only function as part of the story. And if it does, then it will function both at the story level and at the discourse level for the reader who *can* see the paradigmatic reference. I will seek to show in some examples from Mark that at least some indicial elements—if not all or most to some extent—belong both to the story and to the discourse and also that some elements are both symbolic (illustrative) and representational. The analysis of the indicial level will be highly selective.

With regard to indices proper, the "beginning" (*arché*) referred to in Mark 1:1 has paradigmatic correlates in Gen. 1:1 and John 1:1 where the term *arché* also appears. Something of the cosmic and of the notion of a new creation is drawn also into Mark's "beginning."

The baptism of Jesus is a symbol in that Jesus is placed in a paradigm with the servant of Isa. 42:1 and the son of Ps 2:7. Moreover, the baptism is a single element which suggests the meaning of the whole narrative. The opening of the heavens and the divine voice effect a transaction between God and Jesus which is the theological basis for the whole development that unfolds in Mark.[80] At the same time we have observed that the baptism of Jesus is also a sequential function. Thus the unit takes its meaning from the intersection of the line that runs horizontally from the beginning of the story to the end and the line that runs vertically through Isa. 42:1, Ps. 2:7, and all of the cosmic and apocalyptic concepts clustered around the opening of the heavens and the descent of the Spirit.

All of Mark's messianic titles (Son of God, Son of Man, Christ, etc.) are indices, for they refer to a signified—or several signifieds—which was already current when he wrote as well as to the new signified—the new understanding of redemption—which he is developing by his employment of the titles. The titles also are elements in the story, for sequential results issue from the failure of characters to understand the titles which Jesus uses, especially Son of Man.

Events which fulfill prophecy (1:2–3; 9:12; 14:21) and especially Jesus' death as necessary (8:31) are indicial because their validation or sanction depends on an external frame of reference, the Old Testament again.

The meals have already been discussed as an element in the *actantiel* level, but they are also symbols. The particular activity of eating illustrates the whole theological meaning of the Gospel.

Marxsen insists that in Mark 1:4 "in the wilderness" does not refer to the abode or locale of John the Baptist but rather the phrase exclusively and exhaustively characterizes John as the fulfiller of prophecy. With reference to Galilee as Jesus' place, Marxsen takes a less exclusivistic position. Galilee is not "primarily" of historical-geographical interest but rather has a theological meaning. It is the place of Jesus' decisive preaching, the only place where his ministry occurs, and the site of the imminent parousia. It is not that Jesus worked in Galilee but that Galilee is where Jesus worked.[81]

Marxsen's position is too one-sided and fails to grasp how people write and read narratives. The wilderness and Galilee are still places which help anchor the story in the world. Mark may well use them symbolically, but he also uses them representationally.

In discussing representation in Mark we should remember that some of the elements discussed may also be historically referential. But that question is beside the point of my literary analysis.

Precise notations of time are rare in Mark, but they are not wholly absent. After a busy day in Capernaum Jesus is said to have gone out "in the morning" to pray (1:35). The Transfiguration is dated six days (9:2) after the Caesarea Philippi teaching, and in 11:12 Jesus came into Jerusalem from Bethany "on the following day." Mark 14:1 presents a precise chronological note—two days before —and also refers to one of the basic time-structuring institutions of the Jewish year, the Passover. In the section 15:1–16:8 there are five subsections each of which contains a time notice[82]—morning, the third hour, the sixth hour, evening, the passing of the sabbath.

Jesus travels through well-defined places, and the Markan narrative is rich in spatial implications.[83] Jesus is found in Capernaum (1:21), beside the sea (1:16; 2:13; 3:7), in a lonely place (1:35), etc. People come to Jesus from Galilee, Judea, Jerusalem, Idumea,

beyond the Jordan, and Tyre and Sidon (3:7–8). The healed Gera-
sene proclaims Jesus in the Decapolis (5:20), and Jesus himself goes
to the region of Tyre and Sidon (7:24). Peter's confession is at
Caesarea Philippi (8:27). The prominence of Galilee and Jerusalem
is obvious. Jesus goes in and out of houses (1:29, 35; 2:1, 13, 15;
5:40; 6:1), crosses the sea (4:35; 5:1, 21), and walks along the
road (10:32). We observed above that the symbolic may be representational. The reverse is also obviously true. The crossing of the
Sea of Galilee to Gerasa is topographical, but it also symbolizes a
passage to the pagan, the foreign, and the diabolical.[84]

The Markan narrative is hardly one that portrays strong sociological representation, but the latter is not totally lacking. Jesus
has a family with whom he evidently has a strained relationship
(3:31–35). The narrative shows an awareness of different social,
or at least religio-social, class distinctions. Jesus mingles and eats
with all sorts of people—fishermen, tax collectors, sinners, lepers,
the rich, even Pharisees (1:16–20; 2:13–17; 10:17–22; 12:28–34;
14:3–9). Institutionalized religion is represented in the synagogue
and the temple, and Jesus confronts the Jewish leaders, who have
both religious and political authority, as well as the Roman
government.

It is often claimed that Mark was not interested in Jesus' psychology or self-consciousness.[85] This may be true of Mark as a theologian, but the generative capacities of his narrative method, nevertheless, do produce some psychological representation or mimesis.
Scholes and Kellogg[86] point out that Jesus' reinterpretation of the
law as a matter of the heart was one of the chief factors leading to
the development of psychological inwardness in Western fiction.
Might this not have borne some fruit in our earliest known lengthy
narrative about Jesus himself?

That Jesus is said to have seen the heavens opened and to have
heard a divine voice and that he is said to have been tempted
represent psychical experience on his part, however much Mark may
have emphasized the theological meaning of the baptism and temptation. However, this psychical experience is seen from the outside.
The psychological is also in view from the outside when Jesus is said
to be capable of seeing into the hearts of men (2:8) or when his
foreknowledge is spoken of (14:26–31). The same is true of the fre-

quent references to Jesus' emotions—his anger, grief, compassion, indignation, etc. (3:5; 6:6, 34; 7:34; 8:12; 10:14).

We come closer to psychological inwardness in the portrayal of Jesus' sense of mission. He proclaims the coming of the kingdom and in the first person affirms his sense of "coming out" to preach (1:38) and to call sinners (2:17). Here a representation of inner subjectivity cannot be denied. In the garden of Gethsemane we have a still more intimate look at the interior of Jesus' psyche (14:32–36). His distress is objectively referred to, but in his plea to God to remove the cup and in his resolve, nevertheless, to do God's will we are seeing the experience from the standpoint of Jesus' own inwardness.

The most interesting and compelling element in the Gospel from the psychological standpoint is the cry from the cross: "My God, my God, why have you forsaken me?" (15:34). According to Beach it is inconceivable that Mark should have seen this as a cry of despair or have thought that the Messiah lost faith. Nineham has a similar view, suggesting that Mark would not have bewildered the church by making Jesus' last word from the cross one of despair. Both scholars base their argument on the fact that the saying is a quotation from Psalm 22 in which a righteous sufferer affirms his faith in ultimate vindication. Therefore, the Markan Jesus was also here expressing his ultimate confidence in God.[87]

But we cannot really say what Mark subjectively thought was conceivable or appropriate. We must look at the text. Best, on the other side, states that the cry cannot contain the thought of triumph.[88] Nineham concedes that this is a more straightforward and obvious interpretation but maintains that to view the saying as one of desolation makes the narrative historical while it is actually theological.[89] But the saying need not be historical in order not to be altogether theological. It may be literary—fictitious, that is, psychologically representational or mimetic.[90]

The cry does have a paradigmatic correlation in Psalm 22. Louis Marin speaks of the tendency of New Testament texts to refer to earlier texts (the Old Testament) which seem to characterize or relate the very thing being narrated in the New Testament text. When the New Testament text presents itself as anticipated in this way, it both sustains and transgresses itself.[91] Or we might say that a tension or duality is created. This is the case here and in many other places where the New Testament cites the Old Testament. So, again, Jesus' cry is paradigmatically related to Psalm 22 and thus does refer to Jesus' ultimate triumph. But this is what it means for the narrative as a whole and belongs to the discourse.

The saying also functions in the story as a cry of desolation and forsakenness. As a look at Jesus' inwardness it is psychologically convincing. We are made to believe that the Markan Jesus really felt this way despite his earlier sense of having a mission which would be vindicated. I think that the saying's story function is stronger than its discourse function. Our belief that it really could have been this way—Jesus felt forsaken—pushes to the margin of our minds the paradigmatic reference to victory in Psalm 22 (on the assumption that the reader is aware of the reference to Psalm 22 at all). The "My God, my God" is the last articulate thing that Jesus says in Mark. There is probably no point at which the literary character of the Gospel is more significant and the dependence of theology, or even kerygma, on the human word is more radical. For at this point Mark as omniscient narrator (a point to be taken up again) knows more about Jesus (that he is Son of God) than Jesus as a character in the story knows about himself.

Thus Mark's narrative, however theological it may be, is rooted in temporal, spatial, sociological, and psychological reality. Overly theological interpretations—such as Marxsen's view that the desert is wholly a symbol of John the Baptist as fulfillment of the Old Testament or that Galilee is wherever Jesus worked, or the interpretation that the cry of desolation is solely an expression of confidence—ignore the fact that Mark is *narrative* and destroy its rootage in the world.

As briefly indicated earlier, and as referred to by anticipation in the analysis of certain elements in Mark, discourse is the level of the narrative composed of those means and significations whereby the text is a word (*parole*) spoken by a narrator who relates the story to a hearer who perceives it, the level implying to some degree an "I" and a "you." The narrative may be story and discourse at the same time with the discourse level—both signs of the narrator and signs of the reader—being signified in various ways along the story line. On the other hand, either story or discourse may be a fairly discrete enclave within the other.[92] The presence of the discourse level makes the work a part of the reader's mind through the intervention of language. The subject/object dichotomy is broken down, and the narrator (the incarnate author or author as he is for this work) and reader (the subject he becomes for this book) share a common consciousness.[93]

Now let us consider several ways in which the discourse level is signified or makes its presence manifest. One way is by what Todorov calls aspects of the narrative or the manner in which the story is perceived by the narrator. This has to do with the relationship of the "I" of the narrator to the "he" of the story. It is commonly referred to as the narrator's point of view, and there are three basic possibilities: (1) The omniscient narrator knows more and is greater than the characters and does not explain how he has this superior knowledge. The characters have no secrets from him. This is called the vision "from behind." (2) In the vision "with," the narrator knows as much as the character. He cannot furnish us with the explanation of an event until the character has it, but he need not stick with just one character throughout the story. In this aspect the narrator may be one of the characters. (3) In the vision "from outside," the narrator knows less than the characters. He can describe what one sees, hears, etc., but he has access to no consciousness.[94]

In addition to the narrator's point of view we will consider three other ways of signifying the presence of discourse. First, discourse may be *specifically* announced without its being grammatically or semantically coded.[95] Below in my discussion of Mark I will indicate some ways in which this announcement can be made.

Second, *personal*[96] discourse is grammatically coded. The most fundamental expression of the personal is by the use of "I," for "I" has no referent in the world. It refers only to the utterance now being made, the present moment of discourse. Subjectivity is defined not by the feeling of being oneself but as the psychic unity which transcends the totality of lived experiences and is assured of the permanence of this consciousness of transcendence. This kind of consciousness is experienced as I contrast myself with everything else by pronouncing "I."[97] Other parts of the language derive their subjectivity from their relationship to "I" (or "you") in its present moment. The use of the present tense, for example, expresses the time at which one speaks and tends to make the event described and the instance of discourse coincide. The narrator also makes himself manifest by the use of the future tense; personal, possessive, and demonstrative pronouns; and adverbs such as "today," "here," and "now."[98]

Third, *evaluative* discourse is put into play by the use of value judgments, comparisons, and general reflections; by the employment of modal verbs such as "to be able" and "to have to" and by such adverbs as "perhaps" and "certainly."[99]

I turn now to a very selective analysis of the Markan discourse level. Almost exclusive attention will be given to the signs of the narrator. But signs of the reader are also present. Such occur when the narrator reports something which he knows perfectly but the reader does not.[100] Mark 3:6 reports that the Pharisees and Herodeans took counsel how they might destroy Jesus. The narrator knows this full well, and the information is not given here to Jesus; thus it must be offered for the sake of the reader.[101]

Starobinski maintains that every expressive reference to the author of Mark has been excluded and that the narrator is completely obliterated.[102] Probably every expressive reference—reference to the narrator's inwardness—is absent, but that does not mean that all signs of the narrator have been obliterated. Starobinski's argument would be opposed at the theoretical level by Todorov's contention that while the two basic levels of story and discourse are present in different places in varying degrees, every sentence—every word—of a narrative is both story and discourse at the same time.[103] Some indication of this has already been given, for example, in the discussion of the baptism at the indicial level. I would say that globally Mark is basically story with discourse elements being manifested in various ways along the story line and at a few places in enclaves.

Biblical scholars have generally failed to make a programmatic distinction among the various narrative levels and to evaluate and exploit the significance of the fact that the same unit may belong to and hence unite more than one level. The result is partial and one-sided interpretations. It may be said that the baptism or temptation is only of theological (discourse) and not of psychological or sequential significance. Or the general claim may be made that Mark had no interest in Jesus' psychology.[104] Let us recall that the cry of

desolation from the cross is a symbol (discourse) making a paradigmatic reference to Psalm 22, a sequential function growing out of
the event of the crucifixion as a prior sequential function, and an
instance of representation (relating the narrative's world to the
"real" world) displaying an "as if" real subjective psychological
phenomenon.

But let us now turn to some signs of the narrator's discourse. The
latter does clearly have one of the three points of view defined
above. According to Edgar Haulotte, in Mark it is the vision "with,"
for the disciples do not understand the messianic secret.[105] But surely
Haulotte has missed the point. It is not a question of how much a
character knows, but of how much the narrator knows in relation
to the characters. If the disciples misunderstand the messianic secret,
Mark does not. Mark displays the omniscient point of view, the
vision "from behind." The narrator knows the thoughts of men—
that the scribes entertained in their hearts the possibility that Jesus
was guilty of blasphemy (2:6, 7) and that the priests, scribes, and
elders perceived that Jesus told the parable of The Wicked Tenants
against them (12:12). He also knows what Jesus perceived in his
spirit (2:8) and other things about Jesus' unexpressed inwardness
(5:30). Mark can describe a scene which had no witness but Jesus
himself and report on Jesus' psychological state in that situation—
Gethsemane.

We see specific discourse when a signified external to the text is
alluded to as in the baptism, the cry from the cross, and the use of
messianic titles. We see it also when the global meaning of the work
is clearly thematized as it is in 8:31; 9:31; 10:33–34.[106] It is again
a specific sign of the narrator when the text comments about itself in
the form of a summary (1:32–34; 3:7–12; 6:53–56): a new circuit
of communication is intended.[107] Finally discourse is specific when
the narrator gathers teachings of the hero thematically into unmis-
takable collections (4; 7:1–23; 13). Starobinski suggests that the
parable discourse (4) is intended as a clue—for the reader—as to
how the whole Gospel is to be interpreted. Just as the parable of
The Sower is to be translated into another register so the whole
narrative can be read as a drama of cosmic or psychic salvation. This
need not vitiate the Gospel's rootage in history—or representation
—because both the syntagmatic and paradigmatic axes are kept in
view.[108]

That most basic expression of personal discourse—first person narration—is not the way of our author. The story is told in the third person, but Mark does often have Jesus speak in the first person, and other grammatical codings of personal discourse are found. Mark's frequent use of the historic present has often been remarked upon. As an example, the present tense is very prominent in the story of the crucifixion (15:20b–26). The future tense also has abundant expression (2:20, 8:38; 9:31; 13), and the sense of urgency and the pressure of the present are manifested by Mark's twelvefold use of "immediately."[109]

With regard to evaluative discourse we may observe that Mark gives implicit evaluations of awe, fascination, fear, and faith,[110] and makes judgments about the Jewish authorities' state of mind (12:34b) and Pilate's motives (15:15). He uses modal verbs like "to be able" (6:5; 9:22–23; 10:38–39), and through Jesus he makes general reflections: everything is possible for faith (9:23); it is very hard for the rich to enter the kingdom of God (10:23).

At a number of points I have already given some indication of the relationship among different narrative levels. Here I would like to present a few more examples and to state what seems to me to be the most comprehensive and far-reaching relationship of levels in the Gospel. A relationship among levels is established by a unit's belonging to more than one level at the same time or by a unit's being correlated in some way with units on one or more other levels.

First a few more instances of the interpenetration of levels may be noted.

Käsemann raises the question why there was a reversion to treating Jesus' ministry in narrative form after it had already been interpreted by kerygmatic enthusiasm (gnosticism?) and proclaimed in the mythological language of the christological hymns. He answers that the historicizing narrative was a reaction which aimed at restoring the primacy of Christ over the community. This intention could be accomplished only as the expression of chronological priority. The earthly Jesus had to keep the preached Christ from dissolving into the projection of a realized-eschatological self-consciousness.[111]

This explanation of the Gospel form as a response to developments in the history of Christian thought may be true. But the historical development itself, as well as the molding of the form, was ultimately

governed by the generative linguistic matrix of meaning which produces both meaningful historical acts and developments and also
generic forms. More specifically what Käsemann sees in the Gospel is
an interpenetration of the symbolic (the Christ) and the representational (Jesus).

The suffering Son of Man sayings (8:31, etc.) as acts of the hero
are sequential functions, for they have a correlate further along in
the syntagm—the subsequent event of Jesus' death and resurrection.
They contribute to the actant which Jesus fulfills as the self-communicating one and are correlated to the actant which the disciples
fulfill as the noncomprehending ones. They are also a part of the discourse (specific) in that they belong to the signified which is the
understanding of redemption associated with the title Son of Man in
its pre-Markan usage, which Mark is remolding by his particular
employment of the sayings.

Jesus' act of healing (sequential function) (3:1–6) clarifies an
element at the *actantiel* level. The authorities are unmasked and
forced to declare themselves as radical opponents (3:6).[112]

Jesus' conflict with the Jewish authorities is a function of the
interpenetration of the sequential and the indicial. The Pharisees
and priests oppose his (or his disciples') acts (sequential functions)
not because these acts are evil or contrary to God's intention but
because the authorities are malicious and hard of heart (indicial)
(2:6–8; 3:5; 12:13; 14:1).[113]

The Markan narrative may suggest that Jesus suffered a certain
lack of assurance about his messianic role. He is tempted in some
way at the Temptation, and at Caesarea Philippi and in Gethsemane
he is tested with regard to his resolve to be the suffering Son of Man–
Messiah. This suggested lack of self-certainty is sequential in terms
of the test model onto which we projected the Markan sequence
early in this chapter, and it also has a psychological (indicial) dimension, as was noted in the discussion of Gethsemane above. This possible wavering of certainty could in part explain, and therefore also
excuse, the disciples' lack of perception (*actantiel*) as to who
Jesus is.

The index, lack of certainty on Jesus' part, and the actant fulfilled
in the disciples' lack of understanding are correlated with the signi-

fied (discourse) of modern tragicomedy: not assertive nihilism but a questioning skepticism about the ontological ground of things.[114]

We may now observe some connections among the narrative levels and certain other more or less broad principles.

The interpenetration of levels is connected with the three basic types of causality which Todorov has distinguished: (1) sequential causality (an action is caused by another event or condition); (2) psychological causality (an action is caused by a character trait); (3) philosophical (an action is an illustration or symbol of a concept or idea).[115]

More than one type of causality may be operating at the same time. We have already observed that Jesus' death is in part caused by the maliciousness of the Jewish authorities. But we also have sequential causality here. Jesus' actions—as in the conflict section (2:1–3:6), in cleansing the temple (11:15–18), and in asserting his messiahship at the Jewish hearing (14:61–64)—provoke the Jewish leaders to kill him. There is also philosophical causality in that Jesus' death is a divine necessity (8:31; 14:21). Sequential causality is obviously a matter of only one level. But the other two types involve more than one. James' and John's request for high places (sequential function) (10:35–37) grows out of (is caused by) their character as seen at the *actantiel* level (misunderstanding, imperception). They do not understand Jesus' conception of himself (9:31–32; 10:33–34) and the corresponding nature of discipleship (10:42–45). Thus psychological causality here is a function of the relationship between the sequential and *actantiel* levels. We noted above that the disciples' lack of understanding may be partially caused by Jesus' wavering certainty (sequential and indicial). The inability of the disciples to stay awake in Gethsemane is caused by personal weakness (indicial) (14:37–38) which is attributed to the human condition in general (evaluation). Psychological causality in this case, then, is a function of the sequential and discourse levels.

A central theme or image such as passage, departure, or the decisive step may embrace several levels. Jesus passes from one side of the sea to the other (4:35–36; 5:1; 5:21) (sequential). The demoniac (5:1–20) passes from possession to reason, from being an ignorant opponent of Jesus to being a proclaimer of God's act in

Jesus (*actantiel* and indicial). The proper interpreter of the parables (4) passes from the literal to the allegorical level of meaning (discourse). All of these are subsumed under the fundamental passage from death to life which pertains both to Jesus (8:31; 14:1–16:8) and to the disciple (8:34–37) and which belongs both to the story and to the discourse.[116]

A fundamental binary opposition such as singular/multiple may express itself at several levels. Jesus is the singular authoritative individual over against various groups or crowds (*actantiel*). A given text, or even the whole Gospel, may have several levels (4) of meaning (discourse). The many pericopes in the Gospel (sequential) refer to the same decisive step or passage, the same kingdom of God[117]—the new possibility of finding life through death (discourse).

We have seen that the logic governing the Markan sequence is that an initiating action arouses a reaction which issues in death and resurrection. The analysis of the relationship of levels has confirmed the guiding presence of this same theme.

Finally, in this section I turn to what seems to be the most comprehensive and all-embracing relationship of levels. I will adopt and adapt somewhat Roland Barthes's assertion that a proposition of truth is a "well made sentence" (understanding "sentence" broadly) or is the "hermeneutical sentence." The latter has all or some of the following parts though not necessarily always in the same order.[118] Applying these sentence elements to the Markan syntagm will enable us once more, briefly, to grasp the Markan story. Mark is an elaboration of the hermeneutical sentence.

(1) The subject is stated, the theme of an enigma: Jesus is some kind of authoritative religious figure (1:1–8:28).

(2) Misleading answers are suggested before the question is actually put: The miracle stories may imply that Jesus is a divine man. It is also stated that some think him to be John the Baptist, Elijah, or one of the prophets (6:14–15; 8:27–28).

(3) The question, the formulation of the enigma, is formally posed: "But who do you say that I am?" (8:29).

(4) There are delays in answering the question: "You are the Christ" (8:29b) is not an adequate answer.

(5) The answer (predicate) is given—revelation: Jesus is the Son of Man who will suffer, die, and rise again (8:31, etc.) and also the Son of God (9:7).

(6) There is blindness to the truth after it has been revealed: the disciples do not understand, the authorities are hostile, the crowd is vacillating (9:10–11, 32; 11:18; 14:1–2, 63–64; 11:8–10; 15:11, 13).

(7) Revelation is finally effective: in the centurion's confession the crucified Son of Man (8:31; 10:45) is seen to be the Son of God (15:39).

The story as thus displayed is related to the Markan discourse in that in the centurion's confession a character in the story finally arrives at the position (the recognition of Jesus' true identity) which the discourse has maintained from the beginning. The identification and distinguishing of the two levels, story and discourse, clear up the relationship of the existential uncertainty (or hostility) of the characters to the theological certainty of the omniscient narrator. The existential uncertainty and imperceptiveness of the opponents belong to the "imaginary" world of the story while the theological certainty of the narrator belongs to the discourse. The story gives the reader a place in which he can feel at home and with which he can identify because it is like the difficult, problematical "real" world in which he lives. The discourse—and finally the story, in the centurion's confession—points the reader to the world into which he should move. That is to say, in the centurion's confession story and discourse are joined. The centurion comes to the existential certainty which would enable him to accede to the theological certainty of the narrator. To confess at the level of lived existence that the crucified one is the Son of God is to make the passage from death to life.

The final task in this internal analysis is to return in connection with the Gospel of Mark to the matter of the logic which lies behind the narrative, to the decomposing-recomposing impetus in Barthes's assertion that the task of critical analysis is to "dechronologize" the narrative and to "relogify" it. This structuralist position can be related to (some) redaction-critical studies of Mark by reference to Marxsen's contention regarding the lack of temporality in Mark. Marxsen does not deny that the Gospel portrays chronological sequence, but he maintains that the material is proclaimed for the present. By consolidating all of his material in one sermon, Mark unites the earthly Jesus with the exalted Lord who is contemporaneous with the hearers of the Gospel. Thus Mark did not consciously experience time as a sequence of events. Marxsen grounds the possibility of Mark's position at least partially in the Hebraic tendency to cancel time by making the past present through proclamation and cultic celebration.[119] Marxsen also points to the great theological kinship between Paul and Mark—they both identify the earthly Jesus and the exalted lord—while recognizing the difference between them; Mark substitutes the tradition of the earthly Jesus for Paul's term "the Crucified One."[120]

I should like to make two responses to Marxsen which I will then develop more fully in reverse order: (1) He has a one-sided view of the lack of temporality in Mark, and to the extent that he *is* right he does not have the appropriate literary categories for explaining how in fact chronology is vitiated in the Gospel. (2) He does not explain in linguistic-literary terms what it is that distinguishes Mark from Paul.

In Paul kerygmatic statements of a "story" type are taken into the surrounding I-you discourse (Rom. 10:9; 1 Cor. 11:23–26; 1 Cor. 15:3–11; Gal. 2:19–21) and are assimilated to it. Discourse has the power to transform a story insertion into discourse. Mark, on the other hand, is primary story with third person narration, having the discourse indicated in various ways along the story line and in small enclaves. Under such an arrangement the discourse is not assimilated to the story but remains discourse.[121]

With regard to temporality in Mark, Marxsen has an either/or rather than a both/and position. He assumes that Mark must have either experienced temporality or not and he argues that he did not.[122] Actually we are in no position to talk about what Mark experienced, but we can talk about what the text means. Marxsen's fault is his failure to distinguish syntagm and paradigm and to see their dialectical relationship which makes possible a both/and position. There is a sense in which resurrection, proclamation, and parousia are identified in Mark,[123] but in that they are paradigmatic correlates or synonyms. Such paradigmatic connections do tend to elevate meaning above temporality, logos above mythos. But these events are syntagmatically distinguished and separated; therefore, there is temporality in Mark.

Again, the repetition or paralleling of similar sequences, which is typical of all narrative,[124] works against temporality. In Mark the death and resurrection of the Son of Man are anticipated in the Eucharistic story, in the Son of Man sayings, and in all of the many transformed ways in which the conflict-death-resurrection sequence (figure #9) appears. According to Louis Marin this phenomenon of repetition causes the historical referent of a discourse to disappear as the discourse—through paralleling—becomes its own referent. Specifically in Mark the Eucharistic *word* replaces the body.[125] Robert Scholes in speaking about the very contemporary novel—the novel more influenced by structuralism than by existentialism—has pointed to the emerging view of time which sees all life as parallel: time is a fallacy; existence is without history, is always now.[126] Similarly, if surprisingly, Starobinski speaks of temporality in Mark as being a part of the work's *synchronic* system and refers to the quasi-simultaneity of its parts despite its sequential organization. What he apparently means by this is that all of the episodes that comprise the sequence mean the same thing.[127]

Now this tendency to dissolve time and to dissipate the connection between language and its historical referent calls into question the connection between narrative form and the temporality—or "chronologicality"—of existence, which theologians often assume.[128] The use of the narrative form does not assure that all characters (people) are different and that the new emerges. Does narrative have some special function and meaning that another genre could not actualize just as well? If only the communication of concepts were involved, the early church could have got along just with sayings collections, revelation discourses, and letters. I argued in Chapter III that the Markan narrative was a bulwark against gnosticism and the gnostic tendency in realized apocalyptic. But is narrative the only such protection? Narrative at least shows that the paradigm event of death and resurrection must be lived over and over in a changing historical continuum. But Paul says that non-narratively by affirming that he dies and rises with Christ daily (Gal. 2:19–20; 2 Cor. 4:7–11; 1 Cor. 15:31); it is an ongoing changing experience. If it can be shown that any narrative can be resolved into the logic behind it, then it may be questionable whether narrative as narrative does really have a meaning inherently different from other New Testament genres. Perhaps we must turn to the realm of aesthetic experience for the significance of narrative. It may have a power to absorb us in its world of meaning which non-narrative genres do not have.

But I do not really believe that we need to abandon the significance of narrative to a flight into aestheticism. It may be relevant to point out that content, as well as form, is important for meaning. The realistic historical and representational content of Mark distinguishes it from letters, sayings collections, and revelation discourses. As we have observed, the structure is different from Paul's (brief) narrative kerygmatic statements (Mark is primary story with discourse signified along the story line, not discourse which surrounds and assimilates bits of story). This is important if linguistic form or structure conditions thought and self-understanding and hence existence itself. In order to conclude this discussion and chapter let us turn to a particular point of Markan interpretation in light of the Markan genre

B. Mark and Its Genre

Theodore Weeden maintains that in Mark Jesus completely and irrevocably repudiates the disciples. They are not even to be rehabilitated by the resurrected Christ.[129] Such a view is based on the syntagm of Jesus' relationship with his disciples, based on the linear plot as it stands, and this may be schematized as follows: (1) Jesus calls and chooses the disciples; (2) they fail to recognize who he is; (3) then they misconceive his nature; (4) finally they abandon him; (5) Jesus irrevocably repudiates the disciples, or at least Mark pictures them as repudiated. (See figure #16.) This is a dimension of the story which cannot be ignored. It belongs to the texture of Mark's *myth* or plot. Yet in the Markan apocalyptic discourse in chapter 13 four of the disciples clearly represent the church of the future.[130]

FIGURE #16

syntagm ⟶

1	2	3	4	5
Jesus chooses disciples	they fail to recognize him	they mis-conceive his messiahship	they abandon him	he completely repudiates them

FIGURE #17

syntagm →

	1	2	3	4	5	6	7	8
		agon / "death" of hero / sacrifices	resurrection or victory			second agon	defeat of alazon (boaster)	Komos: victory of hero
Aristophanes (synthetic)	conflict	"death" of hero / sacrifices	resurrection or victory	parabasis	feast	conflict	defeat of alazon (boaster)	Komos: victory of hero
Mark	Jesus' verbal conflict with hostile authorities	threat of death	victory in debate and assertion of authority / sight to the blind	Caesarea Philippi	Lord's Supper	conflict with hostile authorities	Jesus' death	resurrection as ever present word
						conflict with non comprehending disciples	word hardens, lose life / repudiation of disciples (alazons)	word gives life, save life / possibility of renewal
1 Cor. 1:17–2:5	conflict between the word of the cross and the wisdom of the world	death of Jesus (2:8) / rejection of the word	power of word			conflict between ironical God and boastful world	ironical God (word) shatters boastful world	gaining of life and true wisdom for world through the word
Deuteronomy	Moses' struggle with Israel and with God for Israel	sacrifices / Moses' death "for Israel"	Moses' life-giving word confronts Israel after his death		festivals	conflict between God (word) and Israel	Israel is destroyed	Israel is given life by the word
Romans 6:3–10						Christ's struggle with sin / man's struggles with sin	Christ's death / death of sinful self	Christ's resurrection / life and future resurrection

paradigm ←

What emerges if we consider the generic *logos* of Mark, the structure[131] to which it belongs?[132] Before attempting an answer to that question we must consider another opinion of Weeden regarding Mark's theology. For Mark Jesus is risen, but the risen Christ is not here; he is not on earth acting among men or in the church; not even in a mystical sense is he present (16:6). Rather the church's guiding intercessor is the Holy Spirit (13:11).[133]

Over against this I should like to suggest that in Mark the resurrected Christ is reinterpreted as the word of Christ. Word is one of the signifieds for the signifier *resurrection of Jesus*. Arriving at this conclusion results from looking at certain elements in the syntagm of Mark in the light of their intra-Markan paradigms (figure #9) and from viewing the whole of Mark as a transformation in its genre-structure (see figure #17). Recall that in order to discover the logic which lies behind and to some degree governs the temporal form of the narrative it is permissible, and even necessary, to rearrange some of the elements. In this way the structure, which is the genre, is built up, and if a work is seen to belong to a certain genre, then the details can reasonably be expected to follow the principles of that genre,[134] though with transformations. For example, in Aristophanes death has been transformed into a debating attack on the hero and into a sacrifice and/or feast. However, in Mark while we have a debating attack, we also have the literal death of Jesus and the existential or literal death of his followers.

In Mark Jesus' word is authoritative (1:22). It has the power to heal (1:41; 2:11), to exorcise demons (5:8, 13; 9:25–26), to open ears (7:34), to forgive sins (2:5), and to give life (5:41–42). It also has power to harden the heart of man (4:11–12). And the word of Christ does not pass away (13:31). This in itself suggests that Jesus' resurrection is reinterpreted as his ever present word, and internal structural analysis confirmed that judgment; the latter is given further weight by the fact that in the resurrection paradigm of the genre (figure #17) resurrection is seen as the powerful word. Moreover, paradigms 7 and 8 suggest that God (or Christ) as powerful word kills in order to make alive. In Mark the content of one of Jesus' most prominent words to his disciples is that of life through death (8:35).

Thus in Mark at the syntagmatic level the disciples are repudiated.

But at the paradigmatic and structural level (both intra-Markan and generic) the *ever present* word which kills in order to make alive and which leads through death to life is as available to the hardened and rejected disciples—and to the Jewish crowds and authorities—as to anyone else, and thus their situation is not hopeless. There is, then, some tension between the implications of Mark's literary form and those of the governing structures. But it is not the tension between tradition and redaction of which redaction criticism speaks. It is rather a tension at the valuational, internal level, a tension within the viewpoint of the narrator or "incarnate author" and between Mark, as a particular transformation, and its genre, a tension between syntagm and paradigm. Such tension is possible because a writer is not always equally attentive to all aspects and implications of his work.

Must we choose one pole of the tension or the other? The organic unity of the plot structure has long been well argued, and the temporality of the biblical story—on theological grounds—can hardly be given up without great loss. On the other hand, I think that the interpretive fruitfulness of structural analysis has been demonstrated. The point at which I am trying to arrive has already been anticipated. In Chapter I, I gave a hesitating acceptance to the view that the task of criticism is to dechronologize the narrative and dispel the chronological illusion. Then in Chapter III I emphasized the temporality, even chronology, in Mark, while in Chapter IV I have returned to consider that logos (meaning) may be more primary than mythos (action in time, the temporal form of an individual story). Perhaps it is vanity on my part, or simply obtuseness, but I do not think that these shifts are mere vacillation. I believe that they point to the difficulty of the problem. Diachrony (or chronology) is not so escapable or so unintelligible as some structuralists have thought, and the cultic celebration of the past in the present does not simply cancel out time as sequence as Marxsen has suggested. It has been convincingly argued[135] that the integrity of chronology—past and present distinguished—is maintained in the Old Testament although a reality or quality of existence which came into the historical stream, through one event may be actualized later in another event, such as a cultic celebration of the earlier event. But the earlier event is not repeated. On the other hand, the simple fact of narrative does not so inevitably carry with it the view that existence is lived as an orderly and meaningful continuum as some biblical scholars have thought. My still provisional conclusion will not be new, profound, or startling.

Events could happen in chronological succession without language, but meaningful chronology—history—is possible only through the language which enables us to grasp the succession of events in some kind of categories. Therefore, it would seem that history as meaningful—the events themselves or the narrative about them—is dependent on the ontologically prior matrix of generative linguistic competence. If history, or narrative, is meaningful, then the meaning can be expressed in non-narrative form. In the Bible in general, and in Mark in particular, story and meaning are closely wed. But a distinction between narrative and its meaning system may not be so difficult to make or so inimical to the "biblical conception of history" as has often been thought.

The two dimensions—story (temporality or succession) and logos (meaning)—are both distinguished and related by superseding the linear representation of a story—such as Mark—or the linear representation of the biblical conception of time in favor of a grid of syntagms and paradigms. Its paradigm contributes to the meaning of any element in a syntagm and stretches that meaning in various ways; and the grid as a whole—the formalization of the generative linguistic matrix—provides a relevant vantage point from which to see the whole syntagm. It is not the syntagm alone which determines the meaning of elements or functions, but the syntagm may determine what element in the paradigm is the presiding one in a particular story. For example, in Mark the resurrection is seen as all of the things in the "resurrection" paradigm (see figure #9) and they in turn make it manifest. But the role of the resurrection itself may suggest that it is the clue to and the possibility of the other elements in that paradigm.

The syntagm preserves the temporality of existence—in Mark, the ongoing reliving of the death and resurrection in sequence—in a way that a non-narrative form could not, simply because it puts one event after another and locks them into each other organically so that one does not escape too quickly from events to meaning. At the same time the events in their order are intelligible only because they express a logic or meaning which is resident in the paradigms and in the structure as a whole and which may be expressed in non-narrative form. For Mark the new does emerge on the syntagmatic axis. During the ministry of John the Baptist time is empty and waiting to be filled. With the initiation of Jesus' ministry it does begin to be filled (1:14–15), which gives to man a new beginning (10:15). For the main line of New Testament thought Jesus' ministry is the new and decisive event; to respond to it is to be a new creation (2 Cor. 5:17) and to sing a new song (Rev. 14:3).[136] But the new acts and songs of new creations are intelligible through the logic of the generative linguistic matrix.

NOTES TO CHAPTER IV

1. See Louis Marin, "Essai d'analyse structurale d'un récit-parabole: Matthieu 13:1–23," *Etudes Théologiques et Religieuses* 46 (1971):38, 46, 48–49.

2. See Roland Barthes, *S/Z* (Paris: Editions du Seuil, 1970), pp. 14–16; there would be a veritable infinity of possible readings for the kind of open text which should be written today *(S/Z*, pp. 10, 19, 22–23).

3. See Roland Barthes, "Introduction à l'analyse structurale des récits," *Communications* 8 (1966): 4–6; François Bovon, "Le structuralisme français et l'exégèse biblique," *Analyse Structurale et Exégèse Biblique* (Neuchâtel: Delachaux et Niestlé, 1971), pp. 22–23.

4. Barthes, "Introduction," pp. 4, 9, 25–26; Tzvetan Todorov, "Les catégories du récit littéraire," p. 125; Marin, "Essai," p. 47.

5. See Robert Scholes and Robert Kellogg, *The Nature of Narrative* (New York: Oxford University Press, 1971), p. 4; Claude Bremond, "La logique des possibles narratifs," *Communications* 8 (1966): 62; Gérard Genette, "Frontières du récit," *Communications* 8 (1966): 152.

6. Todorov, "Catégories," p. 126; "Poétique," *Qu'est-ce que le structuralisme?* ed. François Wahl (Paris: Editions du Seuil, 1968), p. 108; Genette, "Frontières," pp. 159–162; Barthes, "Introduction," pp. 18–19.

7. See Barthes, "Introduction," pp. 5–6; "La lutte avec l'ange: Analyse textuelle de Genèse 32:23–33," in *Analyse Structurale et Exégèse Biblique* (Neuchâtel: Delachaux et Niestlé, 1971), pp. 29–30.

8. See Eugenio Donato, "The Two Languages of Criticism," *The Languages of Criticism and the Sciences of Man*, ed. R. Macksey and E. Donato (Baltimore and London: Johns Hopkins Press, 1970), pp. 90, 97.

9. See Paul Ricoeur, *De l'interprétation* (Paris: Editions du Seuil, 1965), pp. 51–54. I think that Maurice Merleau-Ponty would be of essentially the some position; see *Phenomenology of Perception*, trans. C. Smith (London: Routledge and Kegan Paul, 1967), pp. 9, 22, 30, 132.

10. Georges Poulet, "Criticism and the Experience of Interiority," *The Languages of Criticism and the Sciences of Man*, pp. 70–71.

11. Barthes, "Introduction," pp. 7–14; "Lutte," pp. 29–30; Todorov, "Catégories," p. 125.

12. Barthes, "Introduction," pp. 7–8, 23.

13. Starobinski, "The Struggle with Legion: A Literary Analysis of Mark 5:1–20," trans. D. Via, *New Literary History* 4, no. 2 (Winter, 1973): 332.

14. See Scholes and Kellogg, *Narrative,* pp. 212, 223–226.

15. Barthes, "Lutte," p. 32.

16. Bremond, "La Logique des possibles narratifs," pp. 60–63.

17. See Pierre Geoltrain, "La violation du Sabbat: Une lecture de Marc 3:1–6," *Foi et Vie* 69, no. 3 (May-June, 1970): 79–80. The test motif was developed by V. Propp in *Morphology of the Folktale* and refined by others including A. J. Greimas, *Sémantique Structurale,* pp. 196–197.

18. As in T. A. Burkill, *Mysterious Revelation: An Examination of the Philosophy of St. Mark's Gospel* (Ithaca: Cornell University Press, 1963), pp. 159–164.

19. As in Philipp Vielhauer, "Erwägungen zur Christologie des Markusevan-

geliums," *Zeit und Geschichte,* ed. E. Dinkler (Tübingen: J. C. B. Mohr, 1964), pp. 162–163.

20. Vielhauer, "Christologie," pp. 160–164, 166–168.

21. Todorov, "Catégories," p. 128.

22. Note the distinction between this grid and those grids which relate one complete text to other complete texts, grids which represent the genre-structure.

23. Edgar Haulotte suggests that each unit in a Gospel is a mirror where the whole configuration is present. That is why the unit was retained. See Haulotte, "Lisibilité des écritures," *Langages* 22 (June, 1971): 104. Perhaps we should say that Mark *used* the units because he sensed the structural relationship between the units and the genre which was generating his work, and/or that the genre shaped the units as well as the whole as Mark wrote, and/or that the genre had shaped the units before they came to Mark.

24. Francis Cornford, *The Origin of Attic Comedy* (Cambridge: Cambridge University Press, 1934), pp. 2–3, 71, 74.

25. James M. Robinson, *The Problem of History in Mark* (London: SCM Press, 1957), pp. 43–46.

26. Ernest Best, *The Temptation and the Passion* (Cambridge: Cambridge University Press, 1965), pp. 18–29, 181; Joachim Rohde (*Rediscovering the Teaching of the Evangelists* [Philadelphia: Westminster Press, 1968], pp. 143–144) is also critical of Robinson on this point.

27. Best, *Temptation,* p. 22.

28. See D. E. Nineham, *The Gospel of St. Mark* (Baltimore: Penguin Books, 1967), p. 172.

29. Dan O. Via, Jr., *The Parables* (Philadelphia: Fortress Press, 1967), pp. 198–205.

30. Bremond, "La Logique des possibles narratifs," p. 61.

31. See ibid.

32. Ibid., pp. 73–74.

33. Ibid., p. 65.

34. Ibid., p. 72.

35. Ibid., pp. 72–73.

36. Ibid., p. 64.

37. Ibid., p. 64.

38. See Barthes, "Introduction," pp. 16–17; "Lutte," pp. 29, 36–37; Geoltrain, "La violation du Sabbat," pp. 72, 78–79. A. J. Greimas developed this model in *Sémantique Structurale,* pp. 172–192.

39. See Geoltrain, "La violation du Sabbat," pp. 84–85, 87.

40. See ibid., p. 74.

41. See Sherman E. Johnson, *The Gospel According to Saint Mark* (London: Adam and Charles Black, 1960), p. 47.

42. See Schweizer, *The Good News according to Mark,* trans. D. H. Madvig (Richmond: John Knox Press, 1970), p. 48.

43. See ibid.; Nineham, *Gospel of St. Mark,* pp. 74–75. Burkill, *Revelation,* p. 35. While Mark does not give us a great deal of the content of Jesus' teaching, in comparison with Matthew and Luke, he emphasizes that teaching was a characteristic and central role of Jesus (as in 10:1). See especially Best, *Temptation,* pp. 71–75, 81.

44. For a development of the theme of Jesus' singularity see Starobinski, "The Struggle with Legion," pp. 340–341.

45. See Cornford, *Attic Comedy,* pp. 136–138.

46. See Claude Lévi-Strauss, *The Raw and the Cooked,* trans. J. and D. Weightman (New York: Harper & Row, 1970), p. 199; Roland Barthes, "L'analyse structurale du récit: à propos d'Actes 10–11," *Recherches de Science Religieuse* 58, no. 1 (January-March, 1970): 31. A code may be composed of topographical or chronological items, historical references, names, rhetorical and linguistic devices, actions, etc. The meals in Mark are a type of action code. See Barthes, "Analyse structurale," pp. 26–31.

47. Barthes, "Lutte," p. 37.

48. Even in the first half of Mark certain small "crowds" (in addition to the Jewish authorities) are hostile to Jesus. This is true of his friends and relatives (3:21, 31–35), the people of Gerasa (5:14, 17), and the Nazarenes (6:1–6). None of these are prepared to see the action of God in the ordinary and familiar, or even in the extraordinary.

49. Burkill, *Revelation,* pp. 62–67; Nineham, *Gospel of St. Mark,* p. 113.

50. Schweizer, *Mark,* p. 52; Nineham, *Gospel of St. Mark,* pp. 74–75, 119. A comparison of notes 49 and 50 shows that Nineham interprets the crowd's response in two different ways.

51. Theodore J. Weeden, *Mark—Traditions in Conflict* (Philadelphia: Fortress Press, 1971), pp. 22–23.

52. See Best, *Temptation,* p. 88.

53. See Geoltrain, "La violation du Sabbat," pp. 72–74, 84.

54. See Cornford, *Attic Comedy,* pp. 57–60.

55. Mark 6:30 is the only place in the Gospel where the twelve are called apostles; see Schweizer, *Mark,* p. 135.

56. See Cornford, *Attic Comedy,* pp. 136–140.

57. See Weeden, *Mark,* pp. 52, 62, 148, 162–163.

58. See David J. Hawkin, "The Incomprehension of the Disciples in the Markan Redaction," *Journal of Biblical Literature* 91, no. 4 (December, 1972): 495.

59. Norman R. Petersen, Jr., "So-Called Gnostic Type Gospels and the Question of the Genre 'Gospel' " (unpublished paper, 1970), pp. 65–67.

60. Wilhelm Wrede deserves the credit for developing this view. It has been held by many others including: Rudolf Bultmann, *Theology of the New Testament* I, trans. K. Grobel (New York: Charles Scribner's Sons, 1951), p. 32; Burkill, *Revelation,* pp. 2–3, 69.

61. See Hans Conzelmann, "Present and Future in the Synoptic Tradition," trans. J. Wilson, *Journal for Theology and the Church* 5, ed. R. Funk (New York: Harper & Row, 1968), pp. 42–43; Hans Dieter Betz, "Jesus as Divine Man," *Jesus and the Historian,* ed. F. T. Trotter (Philadelphia: Westminster Press, 1968), pp. 123–125; Petersen, "So-Called Gnostic Type Gospels," pp. 66–67.

62. See William C. Robinson, Jr., "The Quest for Wrede's Secret Messiah," *Interpretation* 27, no. 1 (January, 1973): 19–24.

63. Vielhauer, "Christologie," pp. 157–159.

64. See W. C. Robinson, "The Quest," pp. 19–20: T. A. Burkill, *New Light on the Earliest Gospel* (Ithaca: Cornell University Press, 1972), pp. 16–17.

65. See Schweizer, *Mark,* pp. 55–56, 85–94, 185; Nineham, *Gospel of St. Mark,* p. 32.

66. W. C. Robinson, "The Quest," pp. 23–26.

67. See Nineham, *Gospel of St. Mark,* p. 134.

68. Schuyler Brown, "The Secret of the Kingdom of God," *Journal of Biblical Literature* 92, no. 1 (March, 1973): 61, 68–69.

69. I argued above for the close relationship between Jesus and the kingdom in Mark. Beyond that it might be pointed out that both Jesus (Son of Man) (2:10, 28; 8:31; 8:38; 9:12; 14:61–62) and the kingdom (4:3–8, 14–25, 30–32) are obscure in the present but will be gloriously manifested in the future. Willi Marxsen (*Mark the Evangelist* [Nashville: Abingdon Press, 1969], p. 58) has pointed out that the kingdom is the only motif referred to in Mark as its content (1:14), and Burkill (*Revelation,* p. 102) argues that the context of the whole book makes it clear that the mystery of the kingdom in Mark 4 is Jesus' identity.

70. Burkill (*New Light,* pp. 123–126) does not see the paradox but sees Mark forgetfully turning from one theory to the other.

71. Burkill, *Revelation,* pp. 242–243.

72. Eric Voegelin, "History and Gnosis," *The Old Testament and the Christian Faith,* ed. B. Anderson (New York: Harper & Row, 1963), p. 76.

73. Barthes, "Introduction," p. 9; "Lutte," p. 29.

74. Barthes, "Introduction," p. 10; "Lutte," p. 29.

75. Scholes and Kellogg, *Narrative,* pp. 82–88. The indices or illustrations in the sense used here would tend to make characters typical rather than highly individualistic. Robert Scholes ("The Illiberal Imagination," unpublished paper, Modern Language Association, 1972, p. 12; forthcoming in *New Literary History*) observes that structuralism is influencing the contemporary novel by causing a decline in "individuation of character and a resurgence of typification." An author's awareness of paradigmatic correlation would tend to produce this effect.

76. Barthes, "Introduction," pp. 10–11.

77. Scholes and Kellogg, *Narrative,* pp. 82–88, 98.

78. See Marin, "Essai d'analyse," pp. 47–48; Barthes, "Introduction," p. 11.

79. Barthes, "Introduction," p. 11.

80. See Schweizer, *Mark,* pp. 37–39.

81. Marxsen, *Mark,* pp. 37–38, 58–60, 62, 92–94.

82. See Burkill, *Revelation,* pp. 243–244.

83. See Starobinski, "The Struggle with Legion," pp. 336, 350.

84. Ibid., pp. 336–337.

85. See, for example, Nineham, *Gospel of St. Mark,* pp. 19–20, 35; Burkill, *Revelation,* p. 4.

86. Scholes and Kellogg, *Narrative,* pp. 165–168.

87. Curtis Beach, *The Gospel of Mark* (New York: Harper & Row, 1959), pp. 112–113); Nineham, *Gospel of St. Mark,* pp. 427–428.

88. Best, *Temptation,* p. 100.

89. Nineham, *Gospel of St. Mark,* pp. 427–428.

90. See Scholes and Kellogg, *Narrative,* p. 163.

91. Louis Marin, "En Guise de Conclusion," *Langages* 6, no. 22 (June, 1971): 124.

92. See Todorov, "Catégories," pp. 126–127, 138; "Poétique," p. 108; Genette, "Frontières," pp. 159–162; Barthes, "Introduction," pp. 18–19.

93. Poulet, "Criticism," pp. 57–63.

94. See Todorov, "Catégories," pp. 139, 141–142.

95. Todorov, "Poétique," p. 114.

96. Ibid.

97. Emile Benveniste, *Problèmes de linguistique générale* (Paris: Editions Gallimard, 1966), pp. 252–254, 259–260.

98. Ibid., pp. 262–263; Genette, "Frontières," pp. 159–160; Todorov, "Poétique," p. 114.

99. Todorov, "Poétique," pp. 114–115; "Catégories," pp. 145–146; Genette, "Frontières," p. 162.

100. Barthes, "Introduction," p. 19.

101. See Geoltrain, "La violation du Sabbat," p. 84.

102. Starobinski, "The Struggle with Legion," p. 334.

103. Todorov, "Catégories," pp. 126–127, 145.

104. See Nineham, *Gospel of St. Mark,* pp. 58, 63; Burkill, *Revelation,* p. 4; Sherman Johnson, *Mark,* p. 2; R. H. Lightfoot, *The Gospel Message of Saint Mark* (Oxford: The Clarendon Press, 1952; first pub. 1950), pp. 32–33.

105. Haulotte, "Lisibilité des écritures," p. 104.

106. See Bovon, "Le structuralisme français," p. 22.

107. Ibid.

108. See Starobinski, "The Struggle with Legion," pp. 348–351.

109. See Howard C. Kee, *Jesus in History* (New York: Harcourt, Brace and World, 1970), p. 127.

110. See Robinson, *Mark,* pp. 71–75.

111. Käsemann, "Blind Alleys in the 'Jesus of History' Controversy," pp. 62–63.

112. See Geoltrain, "La violation du Sabbat", pp. 72–73, 84.

113. See Burkill, *Revelation,* pp. 39, 119–120.

114. See Karl S. Guthke, *Modern Tragicomedy* (New York: Random House, 1966), pp. 100, 115, 117–118, 166, 170.

115. Todorov, "Poétique," pp. 124–125.

116. See Starobinski, "The Struggle with Legion," pp. 348–350.

117. Ibid., 341, 349–351.

118. Barthes, *S/Z,* pp. 91–92.

119. Marxsen, *Mark,* pp. 94, 105–106, 113–114, 131, 147–148.

120. Ibid., pp. 147–148.

121. See Genette, "Frontières," pp. 160–162.

122. Marxsen, *Mark,* pp. 105–106, 113.

123. See ibid., pp. 113, 131, 147–148.

124. See Todorov, "Cátegories," p. 128.

125. Marin, "En Guise," p. 126.

126. Scholes, "The Illiberal Imagination," p. 19. He quotes specifically from John Fowles's *The French Lieutenant's Woman* (New York: New American Library, 1971).

127. Starobinski, "The Struggle with Legion," pp. 332, 351.

128. See Amos Wilder, *Early Christian Rhetoric* (London: SCM Press, 1964), pp. 20, 37–38, 64–66, 78–79; Ricoeur, *L'interprétation,* pp. 46–47;

Via, *Parables,* pp. 100, 201.

129. Weeden, *Mark,* pp. 44, 50, 117.

130. See Burkill, *Revelation,* p. 207.

131. Recall that structure in the structuralist sense is very different from Kee's use of the term in connection with Mark (*Jesus,* p. 127), where it simply means outline.

132. Roland Barthes ("Introduction," p. 2) has stated that either a narrative is a simple driveling of events or it possesses in common with other narratives a structure accessible to analysis. This position is confirmed by Marin ("Essai," pp. 47–48).

133. Weeden, *Mark,* pp. 85, 89, 110, 115.

134. See E. D. Hirsch, *Validity in Interpretation* (New Haven: Yale University Press, 1960), pp. 72–74, 89–90, 113.

135. See Brevard S. Childs, *Memory and Tradition in Israel,* Studies in Biblical Theology, no. 37 (London: SCM Press, 1962), pp. 51–54, 63, 81–85.

136. See also for the notion of response to God in a new song Pss. 96:1; 98:1; 144:9; 149:1).

Index

BIBLICAL REFERENCES

OLD TESTAMENT

Genesis
1:1—143

Leviticus
17:11—61
17:14—61
18:5—53, 60, 61
19:2—61
20:22—61
22:31-33—61
23:11—61
25:55—61
26:3-29—61

Deuteronomy—51, 63, 64, 65, 159
1:30-32—61, 62
4:1-5—61
4:2, 10—62
5:5-6—62
5:6-21—61
6:18—61
6:20-25—61
7:6—61
7:7-8—61
7:12—61
8:1—61
8:3—62
8:4—61
8:17—61
9:4—61
10:15—61
11:13-28—61, 62
11:18—62
12:11-12—61
12:16, 23, 27—61
12:18—61
14:1-2—61
16:20—61
17:19—62
18:15, 18—62
21:8, 9—61
26:5-11—61

27:7—61
27:9-10—61
28:14—62
30:11-14—53, 59, 60, 62, 63
31:28-29—62
31:30-32:2—62
32:6-43—62
32:46—62
34:10-12—62

Psalms
2:7—143
22—146, 147, 150
33:9—133
96:1; 98:1; 144:9; 149:1—169

Isaiah
6—134
6:9-10—138
42:1—143
52:7—90
55:10-11—133

Jeremiah
7:24; 17:1, 9-10—138

Ezekiel
11:19; 36:26—138

Daniel—80
4:31-45—81
7:2-12—81

Hosea—51, 62
5:4—138

Zechariah
9:9—102

APOCRYPHAL

Baruch
3:29-30—59

NEW TESTAMENT

Mark
1:1—90, 143
1:1-13—82, 120
1:1-8:26, 29—75, 117, 124, 154
1:2-3—82, 144
1:2-8—118, 121, 126, 144
1:9-11—116, 128
1:14-15—82, 91, 116, 119, 120, 121, 131, 134, 163, 167
1:16-20—83, 116, 120, 144, 145
1:16-8:26—75
1:17—81
1:21-28, 32-34—83, 116, 118, 119, 131, 133, 135, 144
1:22—120, 160
1:24-36, 34—136
1:25—139
1:27—135
1:29-31, 32-34, 40-45 —83, 145, 150
1:34—139
1:35—133, 144, 145
1:37—135
1:38—83, 146
1:40-45—139
1:41—120, 160
2:1-12—83, 118, 135, 145
2:1-3:6—129, 153
2:5, 11—120, 131, 160
2:6, 7—131, 136, 150, 152
2:8—145, 150, 152
2:10, 28—140, 167
2:13-17—81, 83, 102, 131, 133, 134, 136,

NAMES AND SUBJECTS

DATE DUE